Zionism:

A Love Story

By

Jack Cohen

The cover design is by Jack Cohen.
The two intertwined hearts in place of the
Magen David represent love.

Other works by Jack Cohen: "Amanuensis" (2009)
"Discovering America" (2009); "Trove" (2009);
"Confessions of a Jewish Activist" (2010); Antisense (2014)

www.jackcohenart.com
cohen.jack@yahoo.com

ISBN # 1507801185
Elders of Zion Press
CreateSpace Independent Publishing

Table of Contents

Preface

This is the remarkable true story of a young Anglo-Chilean Christian who went to England to get an education, fell in love with a Jewish girl, then fell in love with socialist Zionism and ended up living on a *kibbutz* in Israel. After many years his children became ultra-Orthodox Jews (*haredim*) and finally the story has a very unusual twist.

The book is based on the memoirs of this individual, who prefers to remain anonymous. Therefore the names of the people involved have been changed, although the details of the story and the verisimilitude of the events and places attest to its authenticity.

This is the story of someone, with no connection to anything Jewish, who for love, threw his fate in with that of the Jewish people. He served in the Israeli Army (the IDF) and lived a very modest existence in the young State of Israel.

The author met this individual some 50 years ago and remembered his fascinating story. When they re-met many years later and he was given some memoirs to read he was convinced that this account should be published as a little known and neglected period of Zionist history.

1. Watershed

The cargo ship m/v *Salaverry*, carrying 12 passengers, nosed slowly into Liverpool harbor, revealing a gray city encompassed by swirls of fog and mist.   Standing on deck, I watched with apprehension as the city was revealed in its grimy sameness and gloomy appearance.   It was drizzling, the air was cold and clammy. I shivered, not used to the bone-chilling cold enveloping me.

It was mid-October, 1947 and I had come alone from my home in Chile to my fatherland, or at least the land of my father, in order to become a proper Englishman and receive an education.   My close family in England was Auntie Beatrice who lived in Wallasey, on the other side of the Mersey from Liverpool.   She was supposed to be there to meet me. I was going to spend some time with her and my cousins, getting acclimatized to this different environment, both culturally and climatically.   I felt alarm, and a vague hostility rising inside of me. Suddenly I knew my sunshine days were over. What had I come to?

I realized that this voyage had been the watershed of my life.   Behind me was the happy, easy life of a privileged son of England in the virtual colony of Chile, where I had been a spoiled bilingual Spanish- and English-speaking child.   Then there had been the voyage, the ante-chamber to life itself.   Now there was this, the future as a staid, ordinary Englishman in gray England. I shivered and vowed that whatever opportunity came along for a more colorful existence I would grab it.   Little could I realize where this simple vow would take me.

2. Background and life in Chile

My name is Elliott Hurst and I was born in 1929 in Montevideo, Uruguay, into a Christian family of mixed English and Chilean ancestry. The years of my childhood and youth were spent variously in Argentina, Chile and England.

My father, Arnold Hurst, had gone to Chile from Britain after World War 1, to work for an English insurance company. After being demobbed from the Army after the War he simply saw an ad in a newspaper for an insurance agent in S. America and since he had some experience he applied and got the job. There he met my mother (who was part English, part Chilean) and they were married in 1922 in Valparaiso. I don't know the circumstances of their meeting.

My elder brother Lawrence was born in Valparaiso. Later, we moved from one South American country to another, as my father was transferred from one post to another by his English employers. I was born in Montevideo, Uruguay, my younger brother Ronald, in Buenos Aires, Argentina.

My mother was quite dark-skinned, a minor feature that was to have consequences. It was unusual for a British expatriate to marry a native Chilean and I would say that there was a good deal of social chatter about this

Coincidentally, my maternal great-grandfather Henry Beecham had gone to Chile in search of new business opportunities. He investigated all sorts of possibilities, including mining for silver and other metals in the Andes. He made a large fortune out of *salitre.* This is a mineral whose chief constituent is sodium nitrate, and which is found in huge quantities in the Desert of Atacama, in the North of Chile. In the nineteenth century, the whole world needed it in order to make munitions. The *salitre* boom ended after WW1, during which the Germans, cut off from nitrate supplies by the Allied blockade, developed industrial methods of nitrogen fixation from the air.

The only enduring business enterprise he set up in Chile was the metals import/export business which he established in Valparaiso, and eventually bequeathed to his son, Edward. When Alfred Nobel patented dynamite in 1867, Henry, with his professional knowledge, immediately understood the immense importance of the invention, and bought shares in Nobel's company. It was partly these shares that made him a rich man. No doubt these marital connections helped my father.

In South America, my father had it made. As a senior executive of an English company, he lived like a king. We lived in Pocitos, a very affluent suburb of Montevideo. There is the evidence of the home movies that my father loved making, from the mid-twenties onward: they show us in luxurious surroundings, celebrating lavish children's birthday parties in a huge, well-tended garden, servants busy in the background. There were lots of servants: maids, nannies, gardeners, cooks. We had a large motor-car --- altogether a very, very comfortable, well-upholstered life, guaranteed by wealth and power.

~~~~~~~~~~~~~~~~~~~~~~~

In 1933, our father gave up this job and this existence and we returned to England. His doctors had warned him that he had a gastric ulcer and the climate of the River Plate estuary was doing him harm. This turned out later to be a mistaken diagnosis: he was eventually found to have gall-stones. This event left my father with a lifelong mistrust of doctors, "they fed me on milk and bismuth for two years" he used to say bitterly.

All this affluence vanished when we went to England.   With what was left of my mother's inheritance, my father bought a garage and filling-station in Staines, near London.   We lived in a comfortable home in Staines, and later in Walton-on-Thames.   We had a live-in housemaid (that was common in England, even for quite modest households, before 1939), but not the platoon of servants we'd once had.

Although he had become an insurance executive, in his heart my father remained an engineer all his life.   He loved tinkering with motors and I think this was a happy time for him.   Now, with a service station all of his own, my father must have been in his element.   I have seen photos of him, standing by the petrol pumps, in the greasy boiler suit which I suspect he wore all the time when my mother wasn't looking.   In these photos he is always smiling broadly, and looking terribly pleased with himself.   I imagine business must have been reasonably good in those days, too.

By age seven, I was old enough to go to a boys' school.   It wasn't far from our home in Walton-on-Thames.   It was called St. Paul's Academy.   My brother Larry (four and a half years older than I) went there too.   Every morning the headmaster, Mr. O'Harry, assembled the whole school for prayers (since earliest childhood, events have conspired to associate organized religion in my mind with mumbo-jumbo). Mr. O'Harry led the prayers from a raised stage at one end of the school hall.   After prayers, the previous day's miscreants were summoned to mount the stage, to be publicly thrashed by Mr. O'Harry. He used a rubber-soled tennis shoe, not the more usual cane or stick. I suppose he may have been some sort of humanitarian --- then we were dismissed, and classes could begin.

Not a very edifying spectacle for a child scarcely out of infant's school, you may be thinking. I agree; yet I don't remember having any particular emotional reaction to this sort of routine at the time. It was all part of the day's work. I think children can be persuaded to accept the most outrageous adult behaviour as a matter of course, so long as they are exposed to it habitually.

One clear recollection I have of that period is of not being able to see the blackboard clearly, and of being moved closer and closer to it. When I could no longer read the blackboard from the front row of desks, I was sent to get my first pair of spectacles. I must have been six or seven.

Our next school was a bus ride's distance from home and had several hundred pupils, impressive ivy-clad buildings, and extensive grounds and playing fields. It even had a school song, which we dutifully bawled at important school events: ...."*Wave high, majestic banner!/ Wave high, majestic banner!/ From the college turret hoary/ Repeat the theme of glory/ Amore et Labore....*" It was run by Roman Catholic priests. Most of the pupils were Roman Catholics, and came from all over the country. It was a boarding-school, but had a few dozen day-boys, including us Hursts.

Every morning, before classes, there was a religious service in the school chapel, which all Roman Catholic boys were required to attend. Non-Catholics were exempt; this included Larry and myself. We had been baptized in the Church of England.   Twenty or so of us would hang about aimlessly in the playground until the service was over. I remember listening furtively outside the chapel, to sounds of chanting, and bells tinkling, inside.

One of the boys exempt from chapel was a boy of my own age called Barry Klein. He was plump and wore wire-rimmed spectacles. As I remember him, he looked like a sort of eight-year-old version of Henry Kissinger. I found him a pleasant, soft-spoken fellow, which made his behavior very puzzling. Almost every morning during break, he could be seen fighting --- struggling on the ground, his spectacles broken in the dust beside him, a ring of yelling spectators round about. His opponent was usually a boy larger than himself. I didn't understand why he was always quarrelling, particularly with boys big enough to thrash him. If anyone had told me he was a Jew, I'd have been none the wiser.

I'd no idea what a Jew was, though I had heard the word used, always with negative connotations. Once at a birthday party, where each of the guests was required to tell a joke, one of my schoolmates told a story involving an Englishman, an Irishman, and a Jew. The punch-line was: "....and when the Jew went in, the skunk came out." We all laughed uproariously, myself included. I might not know what a Jew was, but I did know about skunks.

For the life of me I don't know what prompted Barry's parents to send him to *that* particular school. I don't think he stayed there long. Unless his parents were very wealthy, they wouldn't have been able to afford the bill for new spectacles.

~~~~~~~~~~~~~~~~~~~~~~

A few months before the outbreak of World War Two, my family moved back to South America --- to Chile, which was my mother's birthplace. I think, seeing that war was imminent, she simply decided that Europe was no place for her and her children to be, and demanded of our father that he take us away. We knew that War was approaching. I can remember the day we were issued with gas masks. "A.R.P." (Air Raid Precautions) was a word one heard often. And then, one day --- we were on our way back to South America.

Several years later in Chile, when the war was still going on, and Larry had reached 18, I heard some rumour about his "joining up" (many young Anglo-Chilean men and women volunteered for service in the British forces).   When I asked my mother about this, she answered me shortly and furiously, leaving me in no doubt that if Larry did "join up," it would be over her dead body. War, patriotism, politics: these things were all very much of secondary importance to our mother. Her family was her world, and its welfare dictated all her decisions; nothing else mattered very much at all.

However it came about, in April 1939 we left Britain for Chile. I don't remember anything about the preparations; all of a sudden we were on our way. Things must have moved pretty fast --- I know that my father didn't sell our house, or his business, before leaving. He left my uncle Richard with a power of attorney.

We travelled on the ship "Patria," of the Hamburg-America Line. Why did we travel on a German ship? I don't know. I never asked. This was her last-but-one voyage to South America before the war broke out.   She was a very handsome ship, built, I think, only a couple of years before we sailed on her. Ron and I found ourselves confined to the children's section. Children below a certain age were segregated from the rest of the passengers. We ate most of our meals at different times from the adults, and were for much of the day kept in an enclosure with an enormously high wire net fence. Our keeper was a Fräulein in a white uniform.

We were not ill-treated in any way, and that many parents must have been grateful for the relief, and that the fence was only there to make sure we didn't fall overboard; but as far as Ron and I were concerned, this was unbearable. One day we made a break for it, and actually got as far as our parents' cabin, where our mother was surprised and pleased to see us. Within a few minutes there was a knocking on the cabin door, and there was Fräulein, smiling, ineluctable. We did not attempt any further escapes. There was nowhere to run to.

Looking back now, this seemingly trivial anecdote strikes me as being more significant than might at first appear. In my childhood and youth, I made a number of long journeys by sea, on English ships and Italian; but I do not recall ever seeing anything like the approach to child care used on board the "Patria."

There is one more thing for me to tell about that voyage, I heard it from my mother. She told me that a number of passengers on board the "Patria" were Jewish and that they were without passports. (German Jews had had their passports, and their German citizenship, taken away from them). They travelled from Hamburg to Chile, and at every port of call they tried to get permission to disembark and remain. Maybe a few of them succeeded; I hope so. Most of them, my mother told me, were still on board when we landed at Valparaiso. There would have been nothing for them to do but go back to Germany. I have heard several stories like this one, and hundreds more which are far more horrific in detail. Yet I still cannot tell this story, or recall it, without a feeling of sadness and loss.

~~~~~~~~~~~~~~~~~~~~~~~

Most of my memories of Chile are bathed in sunshine. The climate of the central zone, where we lived, was described in my school geography book as a "Mediterranean climate," with cool, rainy winters, and long, sun-filled summers. We arrived back in Chile in May of 1939, and moved into a house in Chorrillos (a district adjoining Viña del Mar) rented from a family called Evans, who were all away in Britain at the time. It was a big house with a large garden, three dogs, and a swimming pool. It also came with a couple of maids, a cook, and a gardener named Oscar.

Oscar taught Ron and me how to make an *honda* (Chilean for "slingshot"), using a forked stick, strips of rubber cut from an old automobile inner tube, and a bit of scrap leather (the tongue of an old shoe was best).   But what I remember most clearly about the Evans house is that it was full of books. There seemed to be books everywhere ---- marvellous books, too, such as I'd never dreamed existed: "The Emerald City of Oz" (there were a whole lot of Oz books: I read them all, one after the other); "Tanglewood Tales"; "At The Back of the North Wind."   I was a voracious reader, but the supply was inexhaustible.   Never before or since had I seen a home with so many books that were fun to read.

We stayed there for several months, while my parents shopped around for a more permanent home. They finally found one in Villa Alemana, about 30 km inland from Viña del Mar. What made that particular small town interesting to my parents was that it had the King Arthur School. This was a small private school; I don't think there were ever more than 100 pupils. Most of these came from English-speaking families. Before the war, it had served as a preparatory school for boys of the Anglo-Chilean community, who would later go to public schools in Britain.

The war put a stop to that, and some pupils (including Larry, and eventually, myself) ended up staying till age 18, and taking the Chilean state examinations; and the number of Chilean boys increased considerably, though English remained the language of instruction in many subjects. I think that like the priests' school, it was what my mother thought of as a "good" school --- that is, one at which the boys came from the sort of families with which she wanted us to associate. In the event, she proved to be right; it was a very good school as far as I was concerned, though perhaps not quite in the way she meant. I look back on those years at King Arthur's as being among the best of my whole life.

So it came about that in March of 1940, Larry, Ron, and I were enrolled as day-boys at King Arthur's School, which was at the other end of Villa Alemana from our house; about twenty minutes' walk if you strolled, fifteen if you were late and had to hurry, ten minutes if you were on a bike.

Larry, Ron and I were given distinguishing titles in traditional English school style: Hurst I, II, and III. in order of descending seniority. First names were never used. The really good times began in 1941, when the headmaster for the previous 10 years or so, retired, and my cousin James Hurst took over. James was a young man in his early twenties who had come out to Chile from England the year before. He had been educated at a famous public school and had subsequently lived a rather bohemian life, dabbling in the visual arts.

I suspect he was not nearly as respectable as the average middle-class Briton thinks a schoolmaster ought to be (or thought at that time, ideas change in fifty years). This would probably have bothered our mother normally, but since James was her sister's son, there couldn't possibly be anything wrong with him.

The members of James's teaching staff were as unusual, and as unlikely, as himself. There was

Fered Georges, who had been at various times an officer cadet in the Chilean navy, a purser on a Pan American Airways airliner, and Heaven knew what else besides; John Castlebery; Arthur Jakes, an athletic young American, barely out of school himself; and Miss Hilda. Miss Hilda was a German or Austrian Jewish lady who taught us languages: Latin, French and English.   She was an attractive, vivacious, charming young woman, but in order to cope with a classroom full of 12- or 13-year-old monsters, she assumed the role of monster herself.

In her classes, the slightest errant behaviour was immediately disciplined with draconian severity: hundreds of "lines" to write; being "kept in" (i.e. detained in the classroom doing punishment work, during our free time) for hours ---- or in extreme cases, being sent to James for what we called a "whacking."

Even school lessons seemed often more fun than hard grind. A lot of the time, our teachers didn't bother to use the official textbooks.   History (thanks to James) first came alive for me, I remember, out of the pages of Hendrik van Loon's "*The Story of Mankind*" --- not from the history text-books we were supposed to read, which were usually lifeless, dry-as-dust compilations of names and events. I can remember Arthur Trask one day, taking my whole class to his room to listen to gramophone records (officially, I think it was a biology lesson).

We heard a boy, whose name I don't recall, singing Mendelssohn's "*On Wings of Song*"; and Marian Anderson singing a song called "*Softly Awakes My Heart*," which I learned much later is from an opera called "*Samson and Delilah*." This was my first exposure to sounds like these. It affected my whole life. I soon found out that I could get my fill of such music from the radio (Chileans are a music-loving people). We had an excellent radio at home, and I spent many happy leisure hours listening.

Not all lessons were as exciting as this. Mr. V---, our maths teacher, came two or three times a week from Valparaiso. He did his level best to imbue us all with a profound horror and detestation of mathematics. He did a remarkably thorough job; I've had a hangup about maths ever since. Latin lessons, under Miss Hilda, were not exactly enthralling either. But there were ways of extracting entertainment even from these. I discovered in myself a facility for Latin, which I was able to put to good use: I did Ron's Latin homework for him. This worked so well that word quickly got around, and soon I would find myself in Ron's classroom a few minutes before the Latin lesson began, translating the dreary sentences of the day's homework *("The table is long."   "The spear was thrown")* out loud, for the entire class.

We refined the technique to the point where I would throw in deliberate mistakes, to make the fraud less obvious.   I remember the sense of triumph and achievement I felt, when Ron gave me an account of an interview with Miss Hilda, after a written exam in Latin at the year's end:

"I don't know vot is the matter, Hurst.   All ssrough the year, your vork hass been good; and yet your exam results are terrrrible!   I don't understand --- vat happened?"

"I dunno, Miss."

Lessons weren't what made school so special, lessons were only the background, against which the really exciting stuff occurred.   There was always something going on.   It might be the preparations for the school play.   We produced one full-length play a year.   Just about the whole school got co-opted into this operation, whether as performers, scene-painters, stage-hands, anything. We did everything ourselves, guided by James and his team.   Preparations took several months.   The scenery was designed, built and painted under the guidance of James, and other staff members.   The costumes were put together in the school sewing-room, mostly by the Matron and James's wife Diane. I don't know who chose the plays: I think there may have been some sort of consensual process. Nothing was forced on us: we all took part enthusiastically, whatever it was we were called upon to do.

Rehearsals were after school. Eventually, after months of mounting activity and tension, we would perform our play, for parents and friends. The first two plays I remember were T.S. Eliot's "*Murder In the Cathedral*" in 1940, and "*A Midsummer Night's Dream*" in 1941. We performed them at the *Teatro Pompeya*, Villa Alemana's one and only movie-house, which had a stage, with some simple stage machinery and lights.

My brother Larry always distinguished himself in these plays. He loved acting, which he did (as he did many things) with extraordinary *panache*. I think he would have made a top-notch professional actor. In "A Midsummer Night's Dream," I was thrilled to be chosen for Puck. Both of us had our moment of glory, however, in 1942, when the school play was "Alice Through the Looking-Glass" in which Larry was the White Knight, and I got the part of Alice --- mostly, I think, because I had a very good memory, and could be counted on not to forget too many lines in a very long part. The amount of preparation that the production entailed was enormous --- far surpassing anything we had ever done before. I remember one of the vast backdrops; most of it was a gigantic chessboard. The costumes --- Humpty Dumpty; the Caterpillar; the White Knight and his horse --- were marvels of ingenuity.

We performed the play, not at the Teatro Pompeya as in previous years, but in a real, honest-to-goodness, full-size theatre with all the trimmings --- the *Teatro Municipal* of Viña del Mar. The play had had, I think, quite a lot of advance publicity among families and well-wishers, and we had a fairly full house. The tension, which had been building up in all of us for months, was tremendous. One of the clearest, most indelible memories of my entire life is of the opening moment of the play. The curtain has gone up on a dimly-lit stage, empty but for a few shadowy, motionless figures; the audience are hushed and expectant, all of us are poised, hardly breathing, behind the scenes --- and Alice (off-stage) begins : *"Kitty! How would you like to live in Looking-Glass House?"...*. It was as though a great ocean wave had broken at last. It carried us all with it.

The play was a great success. It got a rave review in the *"South Pacific Mail."* The reviewer was perceptive enough to realize what prodigies of cooperative effort had been involved, and congratulated our teachers on pulling it off. Among the actors, Larry and I were both singled out (among others) for special praise. I didn't talk to Larry about it until some forty years later, for reasons which I hope to make clear later on; when we did eventually compare notes, we agreed that that evening was one of the great moments of our respective lives at school.

Days, months, years, passed in succession. Looking back on those days in Villa Alemana, I think that we were, all of us --- Larry, Ron, and I --- very fortunate to have had them. Many years later, Larry used to refer to that period as "Camelot." It was the last stage of our life together as a family; from there we scattered, and were never again all five of us (that is, we three brothers and our parents) together in one place. Larry went off to study architecture in Santiago at the end of 1942, and we didn't see a great deal of him. Ron when he was about 15, decided he'd had enough of school; our father helped him get a job as apprentice motor mechanic at the local garage in Viña del Mar.

This garage was the agent for Ford in the region. During and immediately after the war, there were no new cars (or spare parts) brought in from

America (or from anywhere else). Cruciani's staff had all their work cut out, keeping what cars there were, in working order. When spare parts were needed, they were made by hand, if necessary. As Ron told me later, these were the best possible conditions in which to be an apprentice mechanic. Every day brought its fresh challenge. Ron had inherited a mechanical bent and magic fingers from our father, and derived great satisfaction from his work.

As for me, I stayed on at King Arthur's. After James and his staff left, it wasn't the same; the spell was broken, the magic gone. Under James's successor, it was just another school. There were bright spots; we had one or two exceptional teachers, like Dr. Francis Lake, who had been sent out to Chile by the British Council, and came to Villa Alemana to teach for a few hours every week. Lake was a bit of an iconoclast, which I loved (I had developed a taste for intellectual subversion); he used to keep us in stitches of laughter, wickedly making fun of the windy pomposities of our Philosophy text-book ("Psychology and Philosophy" was the title of one of the official subjects in the Chilean secondary school curriculum).

Nevertheless, he got us all safely through the State exams.

~~~~~~~~~~~~~~~~~~~~~~~

I have no recollection of when, or under what circumstances, my friendship with "Dutchie" began. I think it must have been around 1942, when I was 13 years old. Dutchie was some 3 or 4 years older; he was one of the group of senior boys --- among them, my brother Larry --- with whose help James and the teaching staff ran King Arthur's School.

Dutchie was different from the other boys in several ways. Most of the boys were, like my brothers and myself, the sons of Anglo-Chilean families, with names like Hodgson, Metcalf, Miller, Wood; a few were the sons of well-to-do, often socially prominent Chilean families. Dutchie was neither of these. His real name was Ewald Ehrlich, and his family were Austrian Jews, who had left Austria before Hitler's rise to power. Dutchie's father owned and ran a hotel near the Viña del Mar railway station.

So far as I remember, Dutchie was the only Jew at King Arthur's at that time. You could tell he was different from the other boys, simply by looking and listening. He didn't look a bit "English" (a condition more easy to state, mind you, than to define) --- or Chilean, either. And he spoke English with a definite "foreign" accent, though his mastery of that language was far superior to that of most of his "Anglo-Saxon" schoolmates. Also, he was unusually ugly, with a beaky nose, large ears, irregular discoloured teeth, and a misshapen prognathous jaw.

I also participated in the general name-calling of Dutchie, but one day we became friends. We would walk about together, or sit, after school, talking of this and that. I asked him why he laughed when people called him demeaning names and he said "I've been in Austria and Germany, there we were forced to sit at separate desks and beaten up every day. These boys may be mean but they aren't going to kill me."

Dutchie had a sort of scrap-book, in which he noted down things that he particularly cared about. There was a lot of poetry in it, which we would read together. This was my first exposure to such things --- we didn't read "*The Ruba'iyat of Omar Khayyam*" in English class. I was both thrilled and fascinated. Thrilled, because the difference in our ages didn't seem to be important to Dutchie, and he never tried to make anything of it: he spoke to me as an equal, which no other boy of his age would think of doing. Fascinated, because the world of ideas, of literature and poetry which he showed me, was one of which I had as yet only the faintest inkling.

Both of us were far too busy to spend much time together. Once lessons were over, I might stay on at school for an hour, to chat with Dutchie before going home. When I finally did arrive home, a question would be asked: "Where have you been?" or "Why are you late?" to which I would reply: "I was talking to Dutchie." I was accustomed to being asked to account for myself in this way, and it didn't occur to me, at that age, to resent it. Neither did it occur to me that what I had been doing was in any way questionable. But it gradually dawned on me that, for some reason, Dutchie was not *persona grata* with my parents, especially with my father. Once in a while, Dutchie would show up at our house, for some reason or other (not necessarily connected with me; he might have some business with Larry, to do with some school activity or other). And it didn't take him long, either, to realize that he wasn't particularly welcome. His response to this was characteristic: he began to address me as "Pimp," whenever he knew my father was within hearing (he wouldn't do this under any other circumstances). "Where are you, Pimp?" he'd bellow. "Come on, Pimp! We'll be late!" The effect was --- exactly as Dutchie intended --- to infuriate my father. "I don't want that Jew-boy around my house!" I remember him shouting in a rage.

It wasn't till many, many years later that it eventually dawned on me just why my father detested Dutchie so fiercely. I have no way of verifying this, but I think he believed Dutchie was trying to seduce me into a homosexual liaison. My father never spoke to me about it; but then, he was not able to talk to us (probably not to anybody, not even to our mother) about intimate matters, such as love and sex. He was --- like so many Englishmen --- completely tongue-tied about any subject of an emotional nature. I am pretty sure now, that that is what he suspected: that Dutchie had it in mind to bugger me --- might even (perish the thought!) have already done so.

I can't help smiling, a little sadly, when I think back on this; my poor father, torturing himself with the idea of Dutchie making me his lover. At that time, of course, such a notion would have been very difficult for me to grasp, had I been confronted with it. I had never been informed about sex by my parents, nor by any other adult, and had hardly any knowledge at all of sexual matters, whether homo- or hetero-. In my world, sex consisted of certain simple, pleasurable activities which were as a rule undertaken alone and in private. Since the age of six I had associated exclusively with boys, and all the sex instruction I had received so far had consisted of vague, mysterious hints and allusions, conveyed to me with sniggers by schoolmates no less benighted than myself. Girls were totally marginal to our world. I had hardly any notion of what girls actually were, other than creatures outwardly different from us boys. They lived in a world separate from ours.

I think I would probably have been horrified, if Dutchie had made any sexual overtures to me; just as I think he too would have been appalled, if I had done so to him. That was not at all what either of us was after. What *were* we after, then, you may well ask? For myself, I can answer readily enough --- and, with the knowledge born of hindsight, I think for Dutchie too.

Dutchie was the only friend I had who wasn't my own age. I had no lack of friends; many of them were shared with my brother Ron. Ron was eighteen months younger than me. In our early childhood, this difference was quite significant: I tended to take the lead in our joint escapades. I would be the one to poke a stick into a wasp's nest, while Ron (the pragmatist of the family) stood warily a couple of paces away, poised for flight. As we entered our teens, the difference in our ages became of less and less significance, and we and our friends enjoyed many activities together.

My relations with my elder brother Larry were of an entirely different quality. For the first four-and-a-half years of his life, Larry had been an only child --- at the centre of his parents' world, cosseted and fussed over, and (if I ever knew Larry at all) revelling in every moment of it. All his life, Larry enjoyed few things more than being the centre of attention. Then I arrived on the scene, and --- bang! Suddenly Larry was Number Two. He did not take this demotion in good part. I cannot remember ever being on cordial terms with Larry as a child. Relations between us were distant, cool at the very best, with an undertone of suppressed hostility which occasionally flared into open warfare (in which I would usually end up enlisting our parents' aid --- almost invariably to Larry's discomfiture). I was not happy with this situation, since in fact deep down, I admired Larry intensely: he had all sorts of abilities and talents which I envied. But he made it clear that he despised me and wanted nothing to do with me, and I had to accept this state of things.

I cannot help feeling that our parents have a lot to answer for, with regard to this warped relationship between Larry and myself. Our mother had no scruples about playing favourites. I doubt if she ever went to any trouble to compensate Larry in any way for his demotion to No. 2 (when Ron arrived, down went Larry, inevitably, to No. 3), or if indeed it ever even occurred to her that such a thing might be advisable.

As for our father --- it is harder to say. He was a kind and indulgent parent; but far less so to Larry than to Ron or to me. I don't know if this had anything to do with the values that our father had absorbed from his own family --- perhaps there was some special status pertaining to the position of "eldest son"; but the fact is, that Larry was always judged by sterner standards than were applied to Ron or to me, and more was expected from him. Our father even had pet names for Ron ("Sossidge") and for me ("Twink"); but he had no pet name for Larry.

I also note that while my brothers both inherited the darker complexion of our mother, that made them appear more "Chilean." I had inherited the look and complexion of our father, with the same white skin and sandy, wavy hair, which made me look more "British."

In January 1947 I passed my Baccalaureate examinations. My schooldays were over; the time had come to enter the adult world. I was three months short of 18 years old.

~~~~~~~~~~~~~~~~~~~~~~~~~~

I had no idea at all what I wanted to do with my life. My parents would have liked me to study medicine, and I actually took steps toward enrolling for medical studies at the University of Chile; but soon withdrew, because I didn't honestly feel capable of committing myself to seven years' studies. Nor did I want to do what a number of my schoolfellows did, which was to start working for one of the numerous British or American trading companies which were still powerful in Chile. For an Anglo-Chilean employed by such a company, eventual promotion to managerial status was certain, as long as one wasn't too obviously an imbecile. I think even *that* wouldn't have been an insuperable obstacle, either, if one were well-enough connected. Anglo-Chileans were a privileged class, and they knew it, and made the most of it. But I felt that this wasn't what I wanted to be doing.

I dithered around for a few months, getting nowhere. I did various jobs, including a little school-teaching, at which I was very bad. I drank a great deal too much --- a common failing among young men of my class in Chile (I was very bad at drinking, too: always throwing up). Finally my father said: "I've some money put away in England, and the government there won't let me touch it [*Britain was broke after WW2, and restrictions on the export of currency were very strict.*]. But they will let me spend the interest there, and it should be enough to keep you, if you can get into a University in England." This sounded promising. I really didn't fancy my future in Chile. We began to make inquiries.

I didn't realize, until after arriving in England, just how extremely difficult it was to get into a university in Great Britain at that time. The universities were crowded to bursting with ex-soldiers wanting to complete educations interrupted by the war; the government gave them grants for this purpose, and the universities shortened the study period in many cases. As a result, university student bodies were several times larger than they had been before the war; facilities --- lecture halls, laboratories, everything --- were strained beyond reasonable limits. Only about ten percent of the students admitted were school-leavers like myself. To this day, I don't know why they accepted me. I believe that my former teacher Bill Trask had not a little to do with it.

He wrote me a glowing recommendation to the University authorities; as representative of the British Council in Chile, his word must have carried some weight. Also, there may have been some clause in the University regulations or by-laws, giving special consideration to a certain number of overseas students. I don't know. In any event, I was admitted by the Faculty of Science of the University of Liverpool, to a three-year course of study leading to the degree of B.Sc. in Biochemistry. I wasn't at all certain what exactly biochemistry was, as a matter of fact; but the three years sounded a lot more bearable than seven years of medicine. It was to be Liverpool, because then I could stay with Auntie Beatrice, my father's sister, who lived in Wallasey, on the other bank of the River Mersey. She could keep an eye on me.

I made my farewells and left. The recollection of that journey --- by sea up the west coast of South America, through the Panama Canal, then across the Caribbean and finally the Atlantic --- makes me think of R.L. Stevenson's remark that "to travel hopefully is a better thing than to arrive."

3. Liverpool University and Anne

Auntie Beatrice took me home. She was as cheerful as she could be, under the circumstances. These were anything but auspicious. Uncle George (who'd had a good job, as Purser on a P&O liner, before the war) had died very suddenly some years earlier, aged forty-something, and had left her with a pubescent schoolboy son, an infant daughter, the house in Wallasey, and little else. She had no professional skills that I knew of. Fortunately, the war had made it possible, and quite respectable, for her to get a clerking job with some Ministry or other; enough to keep the wolf from the door, but probably not much more.

Adele, the daughter, had Down's syndrome. In those days people with Down's syndrome were referred to as "mongoloids." Attitudes toward them probably hadn't changed much since the Middle Ages: fear, revulsion; distaste at best. Auntie Beatrice herself eventually spoke to me about Adele. She was at a home in Lancaster: Auntie Beatrice visited her once a week. I never asked about her: all I knew about her was what

Auntie Beatrice volunteered. I could have been sympathetic, but I wasn't; I never raised the subject, or asked anything. I found the subject alarming, something to stay away from. I never spoke about Adele to Bob, either; nor did he ever mention her to me. Having an abnormal sister cannot have been anything but a very negative factor in his life, considering the ignorance and prejudice prevalent about such things. So - Auntie Beatrice had to cope with that situation entirely on her own. For me, it was an opportunity missed; if I'd shown any sympathy at all - perhaps offered to go with Auntie Beatrice to visit her daughter - it might have brought us much closer.

My cousin Bob was a young man in his mid-twenties, in a brown tweed jacket, corduroy trousers, shirt and tie. He was not expansive: "guardedly civil" probably best describes his demeanour towards me (and, if it comes to that, mine toward him and Auntie Beatrice). Many years later, when we could talk frankly, and laugh easily, about this period in our lives, Bob told me just how much of an oddball I seemed to him on that first meeting: foreign-looking, foreign-sounding. We had nothing at all in common, beyond two long-dead grandparents and a language. Here in Wallasey, I could not be anything but a liability to him, an unsolicited and unnecessary addition to his life, as I was to Auntie Beatrice. She had chosen to take me on, for her brother's sake; Bob had no choice. He was stuck with me. "A pain in the neck" was the phrase he used, years later, to describe his feelings about me at the time.

Looking back, I think both of them displayed considerable fortitude.

We all settled down to getting used to our life as a threesome. Auntie Beatrice ran the house. My father paid her enough to keep me from being any sort of additional financial burden to her; but I think that was about all. I was in no way a profitable enterprise for her - just more work, more to worry about. I went about getting into the routine of University life. I would get up in the morning, eat the breakfast prepared by Auntie Beatrice (tea, toast, jam, scrambled eggs made from egg powder from America), and set out for the University, across the Mersey in Liverpool, on Brownlow Hill. It took a bus ride, a ferry ride, and a tram ride to get there. This was my first experience of living so close to a big city. I was very much a small town boy. Liverpool was the dirtiest, most hideous-looking place I'd ever seen.

The city buildings were coated with centuries of grime (mostly soot). The centre had not yet been rebuilt after the German bombs; every hundred yards or so there would be a weed-grown vacant lot – a bomb crater. Quite apart from the fact of being extremely lonely and homesick, I found Liverpool physically repellent. Wallasey itself was clean and tidy enough. But it seemed to be raining, or about to rain, an awful lot of the time.

Bob would go off in the morning to work. He worked at Martins Bank. This should have been reason enough for him to resent me. Bob had done three years' war service, and on his discharge, had applied for a grant to attend University. He'd been turned down. They said he wasn't entitled - he'd joined up immediately on graduating from Wallasey Grammar School, and had never made it as far as the University; which meant that technically, his studies hadn't been interrupted. Without a grant, there was no question of Bob's getting admitted to a university. And here was I, a foreign schoolboy from half way round the world, who knew nothing about war except what he'd seen in the movies, filling a place that could have been Bob's. Even at that time, I was capable of realizing - albeit dimly - that this wasn't fair. But if Bob felt any resentment, he never showed it, or expressed it, in any way. Malice was no part of his character.

Nothing came easily to this family; and here they were, stuck with me. My father, as I've said, paid Auntie Beatrice for my board and lodging, but this barely covered the expense of keeping me. I meant nothing but extra work and extra worry for her. I think the only reason she agreed to take me was because of the deep affection she felt for my father. I wonder how often she regretted having done so.

I must have seemed terribly alien to her: my attitudes and behaviour were very different from what she was used to. To give a small example: back home in Villa Alemana, we went --- the whole family --- to the cinema, almost every Sunday night. So did everybody else. It was a major social event. Afterwards, the young men and girls of the village would parade up and down the main street, and along the railway station platform, ogling each other. A few weeks after my arrival in Wallasey, I suggested to Auntie Beatrice one Sunday that we go to the cinema that evening, and was completely taken aback by her shocked refusal. Going to the cinema was very much *not* a Sunday activity for her. It wasn't for a lot of people, in that part of the world. I found out that although the cinemas did actually open on Sunday evening, it was for one performance only, and the movies featured were not the same as those shown during the week; they were old films, obviously shown only as a sop to the few mavericks who insisted on going. I don't know who the social misfits were who attended these Sunday performances. Cowed by Auntie Beatrice's disapproval, I never went myself.

Auntie Beatrice and I soon settled into a relationship characterized chiefly by a sort of wary neutrality. The last thing either of us wanted was open conflict; we avoided it by keeping a distance from each other (in an emotional sense, I mean, not material; in Auntie Beatrice's little house, we were never physically far apart). We did not become friends; that did not occur until later, after I left Auntie Beatrice's home, and she was freed from responsibility for me. But she looked after me conscientiously. Realizing very quickly that I was wholly incapable of managing my own finances, simple as these were, she worked out a budget for me, and made me a weekly allowance. I felt bound to acknowledge that she was right to do this; at the same time, I couldn't help feeling vaguely resentful about it.

I had arrived a month after the beginning of term, and it took me a few weeks to sort myself out, and find my way into the daily routine of the

University.   Outside of classes, there was hardly
any social life to speak of at the university that I
could see.   Most of the students were ex-service
men (and women), several years older than me ---
many of them with families --- who wanted nothing
more than to get through their University courses
as quickly as possible, and get on with their lives.
They came to the university in the morning,
attended their lectures and laboratory sessions,
and went away.   They were pleasant enough
fellows, but I never got much closer to any of them
than to the point of exchanging greetings, and a
little casual chit-chat between lectures.   When the
academic day was over, I went home too: there was
nothing else to do.

I should have spent the evenings in study, but I had
no idea how to go about this.   Throughout my
years at school, I had never done a moment's work
outside of school hours, other than to complete
specific, assigned homework tasks; in the days
immediately preceding examinations, I might have
done a few hours' "swotting" --- a hasty revision of
the term's, or the year's, work.   But of sustained,
disciplined, self-directed study, I had no experience
at all, nor had I any idea of what I should do;
moreover, there was nobody available to show me.
There was a painful reckoning awaiting me later, at

the end of that first year; but in the meantime, my evenings were spent, more often than not, in the living-room with Auntie Beatrice and Bob --- neither of whom had very active social lives after work --- reading, or listening to the radio.

There wasn't anywhere else to be. There was a "front room," with the poshest furnishings in the house; but I only saw it used, briefly, to receive visitors, once or twice during the whole time I stayed with Auntie Beatrice and Bob. The living room was at the back of the house, adjoining the kitchen. There was a table where we ate, and comfortable chairs, and a radio, and a fireplace. When I got home in the evening, the fire would already be lit: and that was where the three of us spent most of our evenings. The Taylors didn't have much of a social life: they went out rarely, and visitors came rarely.

Bob took me along to the boat club where he spent a lot of his spare time. My father had been a member, forty years earlier, and I knew he very much wanted me to join; and so, when Bob invited me to come with him, I did so, though without much enthusiasm at first. I had no social life of my own. The students I knew were almost all several years older than me, ex-servicemen; some of them had been in the services right through the war. They were good fellows, affable and helpful, but they had nothing in common with me. Some of them had families. All they wanted was to get through with their studies as soon as possible, and get on with their lives. Outside the lecture halls and labs, I had no contact with any of them at all.

The boat club was called "The Liverpool Victoria Rowing Club." I enjoyed it from the start. On Saturday afternoon, Bob would get out his motorbike (a 250 cc AJS, which when not in use, lived under a tarpaulin in the back yard) and drive down to the clubhouse. I would ride pillion: the back seat was a little rectangle of sponge rubber, cemented to the rear mudguard.

The boathouse was on the edge of the West Float, a part of the Birkenhead docks. Here we would ply our oars under the tutelage of Ken Starling, our coach, rowing up and down over the murky, oil-stained waters, in between the rusty freighters moored on either side. In the background loomed warehouses, and dark satanic mills. Grime was everywhere. After practice, we would wash the boat and the oars down with kerosene, to remove some of the oily sludge, before going for a hot shower.

Inside the boathouse was warmth, good cheer, laughter, camaraderie: we played table tennis, sat about, talked, ate supper of toast and tinned "snoek" (a South African fish, which wasn't "on the ration"). Some of the members were young ex-servicemen like Bob; some, like Ken the coach, were veteran oarsmen who had been members since the twenties and thirties; others were youths of my age, students whose National Service was deferred. Here we were all comrades; there was no hierarchy. I saw Bob in a different light, less constrained than at home: cheerful, laughing, occasionally almost boisterous. Bob was a member of the club's premier crew, the eight. They had done well the previous summer in local events (among them, the "Head of the River" race, on the Dee at Chester), and Ken had ambitions for them.

There was a vacant place in the crew of the eight – one of the members had moved away. After a few weeks, to my astonishment, Ken promoted me to the vacant place. He had decided that I had a natural aptitude for rowing. I was delighted. This was like rocketing up from private to Captain at one jump. I worked very hard to justify Ken's confidence. Bob was pleased, too: it made me less of an outsider. The Liverpool Victoria Rowing

Club brought us closer together than any bonds of family.

Early in the summer of 1948, we beat the Royal Shrewsbury School crew, to win the Senior Eights event at Hereford regatta. Ken entered us for the Thames Cup at Henley Royal Regatta – the British oarsman's Mecca. We drove down overnight, on the back of one of Arthur Cain's trucks (the Cain brothers were veteran members and supporters of LVRC), sitting on our gear, the boat upside-down on a rack above our heads.   Henley-on-Thames was a tiny town, not much more than a village: during Royal Regatta week, it overflowed with thousands – particularly in 1948. That was the year in which the Olympic Games were held in Britain. Many of the finest oarsmen in the world were at Henley that year (the Games took place not long after Henley Regatta).

We'd been unable to obtain lodgings (they'd all been booked many months in advance) – we slept in tents in a field, and had our meals in the house of a lady who had at least one crew staying in her home, and who fed them, and us, and I think another crew as well. It was all very exciting. We were beaten in the first round by the previous year's winners, an American University team.

It was an honourable defeat (1¾ lengths): we heard, later, that impartial observers reckoned us to be one of the three or four best crews rowing for the Thames Cup that year. Our regret at being knocked out so early, was offset by the fact that we could now enjoy the rest of the week as spectators, without having to keep up the strict discipline of training. It was a memorable week.

Later that same summer, Bob invited me to join him for a week's sailing holiday on the Norfolk Broads. We had come to know each other better by this time. Bob had got to know that part of East Anglia during his days in the RAF (he'd trained in Lincolnshire, or perhaps it was Norfolk), and told me that ever since then, he'd been yearning for a holiday on the Broads. He had friends whom he could have asked – but he asked me. I was touched, and flattered. I had earned a few pounds working during part of the winter vacation, so I could afford to pay my half-share; it wasn't an expensive holiday. Bob had all the information, brochures and so forth, and he made all the arrangements. We packed our rucksacks, and set off very early one morning on Bob's bike.

From Cheshire to Norfolk is right across the widest part of England -- I think more than 200 miles. We had to get there by evening; the bike was a light one, and could not get up much speed, with the two of us and all our gear aboard. With two rucksacks on my back I weighed an extra 30 or 40 pounds. After a time, the little rectangle of sponge rubber under my bottom became a solid block. As the hours went by, it turned to stone; then to red-hot iron. Hour after hour, we chugged on and on. Our only respite was a short break for lunch. Deep inside Bob, there was a capacity for dogged determination which, when it surfaced, made him unstoppable. Now it took over. On we went, and on, and on. That must have been a spectacular journey, across the backbone of England; and luckily for us, the weather was fine. But we were not there to see the view, over the hills, down into the plains of East Anglia, ever onward. When we reached our destination, the shadows were already long. We got our boat, put our gear aboard, turned in and passed out.

The next morning we got started. As we were stepping the mast, we saw a loose rope's end flapping – there was a clink-clink, and some kind of metal bracket or pulley shot down past us into the water. There was only one thing to do. I pulled off my clothes and dived in. The water was only about four feet deep, but full of reeds, and totally murky.

I could see nothing. Fumbling about on the bottom I felt something metallic. Against all odds, it was the lost part. I shinnied up the mast and put it back in place. Bob watched – motionless, open-mouthed. The whole business didn't take more than a couple of minutes. Thirty or forty years later, when we recalled these things, Bob told me how flabbergasted he'd been.

This event – disaster averted, by an incredible stroke of good luck – seemed an excellent omen to start the week, and we set out in good heart. The combined watermanship of Bob and myself added up to exactly zero. Fortunately, the boat was simplicity itself. It had a jib, a mainsail, a tiller, a tiny cockpit, and a cabin with two berths. Learning to sail it was pure pleasure, though not without its hazards. On our first day we were cooking lunch in the cockpit/galley, when a sudden gust of wind heeled the boat right over. Down went soup, primus stove, the lot. From then on we were careful to moor, before preparing food.

By the end of the week we had learned to make the boat go more or less in the direction we wanted it to, and had sailed over just about every inch of the Norfolk Broads (one lagoon, I remember was called "Horsey Mere").   The weather was glorious, the surroundings beautiful. Liverpool was a million miles away. It was a splendid week. Before we left, I took all the clothes from my rucksack, and stuffed them into the seat of my pants. The journey home was much more comfortable than the journey out.

Another happy interlude during that first year in England was the Christmas vacation, part of which I spent with my uncle Richard Hurst and his family at their home in Staines, near London. Uncle Richard (my mother's brother) had been a bit of a playboy in his youth. At the age of 40, the divorced father of two girls, jobless, and with his inheritance almost gone, he enrolled in medical school. He graduated at age 46, married a student nurse more than 20 years younger than himself, and became a very successful G.P., with a big practice in Staines. I fell in love instantly with the whole family: Richard, his wife Hermione, and my cousins David, Daisy, and little Richard (the last of whom was born when Richard was over 60, and Hermione nearly 40). I seemed a very odd fish to them, too (they made no bones about telling me so), but that didn't bother them in the least, and they took me cheerfully to their collective bosom. I loved every minute of the time I spent with them: for a short while they took my mind off my misery.

For I was, a lot of the time, very miserable indeed.

Here in England I was on my own for the first time in my life. Auntie Beatrice and Bob meant well, and did the best they could for me --- but they couldn't make up for the company, and the security, of my family and friends back home in Chile. England was still an alien place to me. I didn't really want to go back to Chile --- I knew there wasn't any future there for me. I simply missed the familiar surroundings and companions of my youth. I felt terribly, desperately lonely. At times loneliness was almost a physical sensation, like acute hunger.

At the end of the academic year (in June 1948) I passed all my examinations without too much difficulty --- except for physics, which I failed. I'd never failed an exam before in my life, and was very badly shaken. What made it worse was the knowledge that I had very few options left. The University was overcrowded; failure was simply not countenanced. I had one chance to repeat my physics exam: if I failed a second time, that was it --- I was out. That summer, urged on implacably by Auntie Beatrice, I sat for hours every day with my physics books, studying far harder, and longer, than I'd ever done before. No vacation job for me (during the short mid-year vacations, I'd worked at an income tax office for a week or two); my only relief was that week at Henley, and the week I spent with Bob on the Norfolk Broads. By the time exam day came round, I was distraught. My head felt as though it would burst. And I knew that I wasn't in much better shape to pass the exam than I'd been three months before. While waiting for the exam results to be published, I kept turning over and over in my mind the question of what to do if I failed again. Returning to Chile in those circumstances was unthinkable. Sometimes it seemed to me that the best thing to do would be to kill myself.

Suicide turned out not to be necessary. I passed the exam; by the skin of my teeth, I'm certain. I like, when recalling that physics examination, to indulge in a fantasy of a soft-hearted examiner, looking at my hopelessly bungled paper, and giving me a pass mark out of sheer kindness --- imagining, perhaps, that I was a survivor (as so many of my fellow-students were) of the Normandy landings, or of a Japanese prison camp, or of being shot down in flames over the Channel. More absurd things than this are happening around us all the time, and shaping the courses of our lives.

I was ready to enter my second year of studies with a great deal more confidence than I had my first. I knew that the worst was behind me; things could only get better. I felt less of a fish out of water than I had a year before, and anyway, that mattered much less now. I still found life in Britain pretty unappetizing, both figuratively and literally (the food at the Students' Union Canteen, though incredibly cheap, was the most awful I have ever swallowed, before or since). But now I realized that there was a whole world outside, waiting for the chance to be my oyster. Hooray!

~~~~~~~~~~~~~~~~~~~~~~~~~~~

A turning point in my life came at the beginning of my second year at Liverpool University. At the first session of *Organic Chemistry, Part 1 (Practical)* I received an agreeable surprise. The person assigned to the place next to mine at the laboratory bench was a young woman of my own age.

I think I've made it clear that all through boyhood, my relations with girls of my own age were virtually non-existent. There had been one girl (Anglo-Chilean, like myself), with whom I had attempted to form a relationship of some kind; we'd held hands in the cinema, and got as far as kissing once or twice. But that relationship had failed, because of my utter inability to sustain it. Phyllis would have been willing enough to continue it, I think; but my total lack of experience in associating with girls, combined with a paralyzing, near-pathological shyness in their company, made it impossible. With other boys, I could be friends; with girls, I just didn't know how.

During my last years in Chile I'd ended up pretty well avoiding girls altogether. This doesn't mean that I didn't have the normal urges and desires: quite the contrary. The subject of sex was never far from my mind; in fact, most of the time it loomed right up front and centre. But there wasn't a lot I was able to do about it. The means I had available for satisfying my sexual urges on my own, were woefully inadequate. They provided at best some very temporary physical relief, while leaving increasingly anguished yearnings unappeased.

In the society in which I grew up, boy-girl relationships, of the kind which would eventually lead to the choice of a marriage partner, stopped far short of sexual intercourse. Adolescent boys and young men in Chile got their sexual initiation with professional help. There is no shortage there of prostitutes, and brothels of all kinds. They are patronized by men of all social classes, young and old, single and married. Chile is a male-dominated society (in the Chile of my youth, the majority of women --- especially married ones --- were still, legally and by social custom, not much better off in many ways than household chattels). The use of modern methods of family planning is condemned by the prevailing religion as a mortal sin. Widespread prostitution enables married men to get their rocks off regularly, without the risk of producing families larger than they can afford to keep. Most of them seem quite capable of performing the moral and ethical contortions necessary to live under such social-religious constraints (isn't adultery a mortal sin?). What do women do? No one ever told me. My guess is that they do what most women do, in any male-controlled society: endure as best they can, and wait for day to dawn.

Anyway, by the age of 16 or 17, most of my friends in Chile were habitués, or at least occasional patrons, of a variety of brothels, houses of assignation, or whatever. They often urged me to join them; I declined. Why? Certainly not from moral scruples. The last thing I wanted was to "keep myself pure." I think it was fear that kept me away from the brothels. Fear of what? I'm not sure. Fear of women in general; fear of venereal disease, as well. I remember reading, as an adolescent, an account of a survey carried out on young men entering University in Chile: one in every ten, it said, had some form of venereal disease; one in every fifty had syphilis. Not bad for eighteen-year-olds! I knew as much as a lot of variegated reading could teach me, about a number of venereal diseases. I'd seen people with all sorts of conditions arising from venereal disease. One of my schoolmates had had acute gonorrhea, and gave me a most harrowing description of the symptoms.

We'd once had a gardener, several years earlier, who walked with a very peculiar gait, picking his feet up and putting them down in a singularly odd fashion. Uncle Richard, whom I told one day about this, explained that what the gardener probably had was *tabes dorsalis*, a condition associated with an advanced stage of syphilis (In many Western countries, *tabes dorsalis* is so uncommon today that lots of young doctors have never seen it). I knew about the final stage of syphilis, which the books called "general paralysis of the insane."

I have always had a vivid and somewhat morbid imagination, and had no difficulty in imagining myself succumbing to these and a host of other maladies, as the result of a brief encounter down at "Doña Josefina's ." Being also a bit of a pessimist, I was in little doubt that a single excursion into sin would suffice for me to get the whole horrible bundle of diseases at one go.

Another powerful factor --- perhaps it was the most powerful of all --- constraining me to virtue (or at any rate - to continence), was the thought of having to confess to my parents, in the event of my getting infected with one or more of these revolting diseases. I didn't see how I'd be able to keep it from them; I'd need their help in getting cured. The feelings of shame and guilt which I could already sense in advance (not at the prospect of having a disease, but at the thought of having to admit the fact to my parents) were probably by themselves enough to keep me chaste.

Whatever the reasons, the fact is that I arrived in England a virgin; and once there, I could hardly help but remain one. The sight of the tarts on Liverpool's Lime Street was a most convincing disincentive to sexual profligacy, even if I could have afforded their dubious charms; and in my social life, I had almost no contact with women my own age. I did, on one occasion while staying at Uncle Richard's, get an invitation from a most attractive girl, a year or two older than myself, named Chloe. She was a very liberated woman for her time. She made her intentions and desires as clear as modesty would allow ("I've got this nasty big hole at the top of my nylon, Elliott Look!"......), short of spelling them out in as many words; but I panicked, and was paralyzed, and the opportunity was lost.........even now, I cringe inwardly, at the recollection of that dreadful, pathetic evening. Kind, good-natured Chloe! She said no word of reproach; simply, gently wrote me off. All my life, I have been treated by women more kindly than I deserve.

Back to *Organic Chemistry, Part 1 (Practical)*.

There'd been almost no women of my age in the courses I attended during my first year at University. This was due to the structure of secondary education in Britain at that time. A student passing his or her school-leaving examinations at the highest possible level, was considered to qualify for exemption from the first year of studies, in most University courses. Since only the top rank of school-leavers could get into University at all, they all went straight into the second year. So it came about, that to the serious, disciplined ex-servicemen who had been my fellow-students the previous year, had now been added a leavening of cheerful, relatively skittish eighteen- and nineteen-year olds.

And one of these --- a female! --- had been allocated the place on the laboratory bench next to mine.

She was unaffectedly friendly, and disposed to chat. Her name was Anne. She was a newcomer to the University, and very excited about it; and I was (in her eyes, at least) an old hand. She asked me questions about University life, which I did my best to answer with the assurance born of a year's experience. She asked me questions about myself --- where I came from, how I'd got to Liverpool. Chile was, for her, a far-off exotic place. Soon after she'd learned where I came from, I heard her whistling, very loudly, "La Paloma." "La Paloma" is an "*habanera*" --- a Cuban song. I smiled to myself; to most native speakers of English, one Latin American country is indistinguishable from another. That didn't matter. "She finds me interesting," I thought. This was wonderful.

We were both taking the same courses; so we met every day, at lectures and at laboratory "practicals." Places at the laboratory benches were allocated by name, in alphabetical order; her surname was Hoult, so we worked side by side. It was natural we should become friends; she found it easier to relate to me than to the ex-servicemen, several years older. As for me --- I found myself able to relax and feel at ease in her company, in a way I'd never known before. She observed that our fellow students often called me "Chile," or

"Chil," and began to do the same. We spent more and more time together at the University, as the days and weeks went by.

Soon after we met, she told me she was Jewish. This is always a delicate moment. In most places in the world outside of Israel, being a Jew is more often a social encumbrance than an asset (the old Yiddish saying *"Shver tzu zeyn a Yid"* --- "It's hard to be a Jew" --- has many meanings. This is just one of them). Even in the most civilized and liberal of Western societies, the statement "I'm a Jew" can evoke a negative response of some kind, and therefore is best made as early as possible in any new acquaintance, to avoid misunderstanding. In Britain, in 1948, this was certainly very much the case.

Relations between Jews and Gentiles were extremely uncomfortable at that moment. British colonial rule in Palestine had just come to a very messy end, after thirty years of bitter political wrangling, rioting, and civil war between Jews and Arabs (now that the State of Israel was a fact, there was a full-scale war going on out there). Most Britons knew nothing, and cared less, about the political and historical background to the Arab-Israel conflict. They were very much aware, on the other hand, of some of the more sensational events to which this conflict, and Britain's part in it, had given rise. Lord Moyne, a British Colonial Secretary, had been assassinated by Jewish nationalists a few years earlier; and several British soldiers had been kidnapped and hanged by members of a Jewish nationalist organization, which was called by its members "*Lehi*" (a Hebrew acronym for "Fighters for the Freedom of Israel"), and execrated by the British Government and newspapers as "The Stern Gang," terrorists and murderers. These events received wide publicity in Britain, and did nothing to endear the Zionist cause (and by inevitable association, the Jews in general) to the British public.

Among the Jewish community of Great Britain, on the other hand, the establishment of the State of Israel caused a huge outpouring of national fervour. Many Jews who had previously had little or nothing to do with Zionism became enthusiastic supporters of the infant Jewish state, now fighting for its life against the entire Arab world. Feelings were running very high.

This --- as well as I can describe it in a few words -- is the background against which Anne told me "I'm Jewish." I don't think I was personally of any great importance to her as yet; simply another new acquaintance, with whom friendship might or might not develop. It was the admission itself which was important: a necessary, ineluctable act, a ritual which must be repeated every time a new personal contact is made. The steps are clearly marked out, and are always pretty much the same: first, the search for the right moment, and for the right words; next, the statement; then, most important and fateful of all, the waiting and watching for a reaction, especially a negative one. This may take many forms, some of them far removed from the overt, crude rebuff: a slight narrowing of the eyes, a contraction of the nostrils, a pursing of the lips --- all perhaps so faint as to be almost imperceptible; other signs, more obvious: a drawing back of the body, a change in the tone of voice --- an infinity of nuances, in the body language of rejection.

Most Jews who live in a non-Jewish society acquire some skill at interpreting body language. It helps them to avoid disagreeable situations. I think that among Jews born and brought up in Israel, this skill is less well developed (whereas among Arabs born and brought up in Israel, the opposite may well be true. Their position in Israeli society mirrors, in some ways, that of Jews in a non-Jewish world).

What I've written above was not just made up to add some dramatic effect to an otherwise unexciting story. It is based partly on decades of observation, partly on personal experience. When I am away from Israel, people who discover where I come from almost invariably assume that I'm a Jew, and react each according to their nature and education. I have learned to anticipate this and watch what happens. Mostly, nothing very much does.

Occasionally, the results are interesting. There was a hotel clerk many years ago in Mannheim who, after checking me in, insisted on addressing me as "Mr. Cohen," even after being reminded several times that that was not my name. To understand the full significance of this, it is necessary to know that in Germany under the Nazi regime, Jews whose name did not have an obvious "Jewish" sound (Cohen, Loewy, Goldfarb) were required to add "Cohen" to it, thus: "Cohen-Braun," "Cohen-Mueller," and so forth. This young man obviously knew that; even though he'd probably been born long after Hitler's death, and might never even have met a Jew in his life. I confess, I was at a loss as to how to deal with this situation, and in fact let it pass. It occurs to me now that Dutchie would have known how to cut this obnoxious little Nazi down to size.

I have no recollection of Anne telling me she was Jewish. As far as I was concerned, this was a datum of little significance. My education, though nominally Christian, had not had a lot of anti-Semitic bias. The only Jew I'd ever known at all well was Dutchie; and my friendship with him certainly wasn't going to prejudice me against Jews --- quite the contrary. I had encountered anti-Semitic phenomena once or twice.

I remember when I was about 16, the father of one of my friends gave me a pamphlet to read. It was in Spanish, and was called *"Los Protocolos de los Ancianos de Sion."* He told me it described the details of a plot by the Jews to take over the world. I read it. It struck me as a piece of nonsense, and I told my friend's father so. He was much put out, and said I couldn't see the truth even when it was shoved right under my nose. (Years later, I learned that "The Protocols of the Elders of Zion" is a classic work of anti-Semitic hate literature, composed in Russia about a hundred years ago by political propagandists of the Czarist government. It has been translated into many languages, and is still reprinted regularly by professional anti-Semites, in countries as far apart as Egypt and Sweden. It remains an evil piece of nonsense.)

In short: I was aware that a lot of people were ill-disposed towards Jews, for reasons which weren't at all clear; but whatever these reasons were, I didn't see them as being relevant to myself. That is why I don't remember Anne telling me she was Jewish. She might as well have been telling me that she had a birthmark on her left shoulder. It had nothing at all to do with whatever might happen between us.

Or so I thought.

Just how wrong can one get? I was soon to find out; for, as I realized to my consternation and dismay, I was falling head-over-heels in love.

Looking back, it seems pretty obvious that it was inevitable. Take a young man, in the prime of life and physical fitness, socially dislocated, lonely, hungry for friendship and affection; put him in the company of an attractive, intelligent, friendly, approachable young woman. What would you expect to happen? Precisely what did happen, of course.

I don't recall in detail the sequence of events during that period. Anne and I continued to spend a lot of time together during the day. At some point, I plucked up enough courage to ask her to spend some time with me after classes. She agreed readily enough. We didn't do anything very special, just strolled through the streets for an hour or two, talking. I learned that she was an only child; her father was a high school teacher, her mother a housewife. They lived in Childwall, a twenty-minute tram ride from the centre of town and the University. She insisted on going home alone; there was no need, she said, for me to accompany her. We repeated this experience on several occasions. We did other things together: for the "Chemical Society Concert" (an evening of variety-type entertainment put together by students) we were both co-opted as assistant stage managers, assembling props and making bits of scenery. Anne also did a solo act at the Concert, singing a couple of songs. She had a rather nice singing voice.

At some point in the course of these innocuous activities I realized that I had fallen in love. I'd been in love before, of course --- dozens, nay, *hundreds* of times. When I was a little boy of four or five, there were my mother's friends --- like Miss Thomas, whom I used to call "Raspberry-Eyes." Later, there were school-teachers for whom I secretly languished, like Miss Nanken, a buxom young woman who taught us biology at King

Arthur's School.   Then there were the literary heroines, especially those in historical romances. I had a particular weakness for ladies in novels by H. Rider Haggard: Otomie in *"Montezuma's Daughter"*; *"SHE-Who-Must-Be-Obeyed."*   Another writer of historical novels whose women usually filled me with yearning, was Rafael Sabatini (*"Captain Blood*," *"Scaramouche*," *"St.   Martin's Summer"*). Besides these, there was an endless procession of movie actresses, beginning with Shirley Temple when I was about six.

Now what all these amorous attachments had in common, was that I didn't actually have to **do** anything about them: I could adore these females (singly, or two, or three, or any number, simultaneously --- it didn't matter), and sigh for them, and fantasize about them, all alone, safe in the solitary recesses of my own soul, while carrying on as usual with the business of my real life. Nobody ever needed to know about them -- least of all, the objects of my passion themselves (I never even wrote a single fan letter to a movie actress).

But this was completely different. Anne was no fantasy. She was very much indeed a part of my real life ---and what I felt about her was very real too, and growing stronger and more imperative day by day. I couldn't concentrate on any of my usual interests, for thinking about her. There was no satisfaction to be found in any activity which didn't directly involve Anne. I couldn't sleep; I'd lie awake hour after hour, thinking about her (this was the only time in my life that I've ever suffered from insomnia). And the consternation and dismay, which I mentioned earlier, were occasioned by the terrifying realization that whether I wanted to or not, I was going to have to do something about it.

Soon.

Urgently.

My recollections of that period are confused and not in any clear sequence. I think this must be because of the state of intense emotional turmoil in which I was living. I'd never known anything like it. Some of the things I felt, I recall very vividly: the sense of mounting desperation, as the need to make my feelings known to Anne fought ever more furiously against the piled-up inhibitions of a lifetime. Finally biology triumphed, the inhibitions gave way, and I told all. Here again, the thing I remember most clearly is the feeling of infinite relief, at finally getting it out in the open.

Anne must have helped me. I think she had a pretty good idea what was the matter, and saw how heavy the going was for me; and with a woman's generous heart, did what she could to make things easier. *"When pain and anguish wring the brow / A ministering angel thou."* Silly-sounding words; how true they actually are. Sometimes I almost wish I were a religious man, just so that I could give thanks to God for the miracle that is womankind. Women restore that faith in human nature which men work so assiduously to demolish. They make a man's life worth living.

Once I had made my declaration of love, it was up to Anne to respond. She could send me packing with a flea in my ear; or she could answer me in kind: "How wonderful it is to hear you say this, dearest, because I'm madly in love with you, too." She did neither of these. She accepted my confession gracefully, recognizing that I was, after all, paying her a very great compliment, in laying my heart at her feet. But at the same time, she warned me not to make any sort of long-range plans involving the two of us. "There's no future for you and me," she said. "Why not?" I asked. "Because I'm Jewish, and you're not," was her reply. I was thunderstruck. This didn't matter to me, it simply hadn't occurred to me that it might matter to her -- might matter, in fact, very much indeed.

I had not the faintest notion, at that time, of what being Jewish meant, or could mean, to a person. The only Jew of importance in my life so far had been Dutchie. For him, being Jewish had had no positive meaning at all. It had been nothing but a social impediment, an obstacle to acceptance and advancement in the world --- in **my** world, the Christian world, the world to which Dutchie was grudged an entrée because of being a Jew. This was the only world which, as far as I was concerned, had any real existence at all: anything outside it was marginal --- a sort of outer darkness, from which anyone in their right senses should be glad to be delivered.

Being a Jew was clearly one of those things that put you in the outer darkness. And by extension, being a Jew beloved of a Christian would bring you in from that darkness, into the light; it would be a sort of visa, to get you admitted into the real world. Anne should be glad that I loved her, glad of a chance for legitimacy, glad of an opportunity to become "one of us" under my aegis. I don't recall ever having had thoughts as clearly stated as these;

but if I had, I think they would have been along these lines. I was as ignorant as the next man, as to what being a Jew might signify........to a Jew. My enlightenment was about to begin.

Only now, looking back, do I realize how powerful were the pressures that would be brought to bear on Anne because of her relationship with me. She must have already been feeling them, almost from the moment we met. There were other Jewish students at the University. I remember observing that among the various societies and clubs which solicited students to join (they would have bookstalls and information booths open on certain days in the week, in the lobby of the Students' Union building), there was a Jewish Students' Society. I took no more than passing notice of this --- a Jewish Students' Society had nothing to do with me.

But it did with Anne, and with all the other Jewish students. Every Jewish student at the University was a member of the JSS. The Jewish community of Liverpool was at that time one of the largest in Northern England, numbering several thousand; and like all other such communities (in cities such as Manchester, Leeds, etc.) was very close-knit, sustaining a very active social life among its members. Consequently, many --- possibly most --- of the Jewish students at the University knew each other before they ever enrolled as students. As with non-Jews, the university provided a social milieu within which young unmarried people could develop relationships with potential future life partners. From her first day at the University, Anne would have come under the scrutiny of all the unattached male Jewish students, as a "possible." Every move she made would be observed; any liaison she formed, noted immediately. And if this were with a non-Jewish man, it would meet with severe and universal disapproval. A Jewish girl who got involved with a Gentile was disgracing herself --- and by association, the rest of her family --- in the eyes of her entire community.

Anne knew all this before we ever exchanged a word. In fact (as she told me later), as soon as the two of us began to be seen about together, she was approached by one or two of her fellow-students, who warned her that what she was doing could harm her standing --- not so much among the students, as in the Jewish community as a whole. She knew, she told me, that these warnings were well-intentioned, and not meant as threats --- but they must have given her pause, nonetheless. Among other things, it must have been clear to her that very soon her parents would get wind of what was going on.   Yet she didn't break off her relationship with me.   This is indicative of two things: first, that she was developing more than a casual interest in me; second, that she had unusual courage and strength of character.   What she expected to happen, I don't know.   Probably, she didn't either.

It all seems strange now, looking back.   Much has changed in Jewish-Christian relations in Britain, in the last fifty years.   The deep cultural gulf separating Jews and Christians has narrowed greatly.   I read recently that one out of every two Jewish young people in Britain marries someone belonging to another religion: over there, this will almost always be a Christian --- not necessarily practicing, but at any rate, from a Christian family. This situation prevails, it appears, not only in Britain, but throughout much of the Western world, and not only between Jews and Christians; many young people, of many faiths, no longer consider the religion into which they were born, a decisive factor in their choice of a life partner.   The quandary in which Anne found herself with respect to me would seem to many young people today, absurd and irrelevant --- as it seemed, then, to me. But it was anything but irrelevant to her.

Anne's family were Eastern European Jews: her grandparents had all been born in Russia. Her mother, I think, had been born in England, while her father had arrived there with his family as a little boy. They had all been a part of that great migration Westward of Jews from Eastern Europe, which had occurred during the last few decades of the nineteenth century, and the first two decades of the twentieth. The social attitudes of Anne's parents (and to a lesser extent, the attitudes of Anne as well) --- the way in which they viewed themselves in relation to the population as a whole --- were still, in large part, those which had been shaped by centuries of life in the "old country." In the Czarist Empire (a violent and intensely racist society, as Russia is today) there existed a racial "pecking order" in which Jews were at the bottom of the ladder. Jews were discriminated against in all walks of society, and often savagely ill-treated. The Jewish response to this situation was to form a very close, introverted society, with very little social contact with non-Jews; these were regarded, on the whole, with suspicion and mistrust.

When these Jews settled in Britain, they retained the same form of communal organization as had served them in Eastern Europe, even though there was much less need for it. Outwardly, they rapidly assumed many of the cultural trappings --- language, mode of dress --- of their Gentile neighbours; but as a community, they remained almost hermetically separate. Old habits die hard; one, or even two generations were not enough for the complete integration of these Jews into the Anglo-Saxon world. Outwardly, Mr. and Mrs. Hoult were no different from the non-Jewish people among whom they lived --- they looked the same, they wore the same sort of clothes, they spoke the same language. They lived in a home just like those of their Gentile neighbours on either side, with whom they were on good (if distant) terms, and would exchange polite greetings when they chanced to meet. They listened to the same radio programmes, and when they went to the cinema, they saw the same movies. But they still retained many of the social attitudes of their ancestors in Eastern Europe.

Their social contacts were limited almost exclusively to the Jewish community. All their friends were Jewish; when I entered the Hoult home eventually as a visitor, I may have been the first Gentile ever to do so (other than tradesmen and such). Mrs. Hoult spoke Yiddish with her friends, who were all Jewish ladies like herself; they were the same ladies with whom she would socialize at the synagogue, and at her Zionist ladies' club. Mr. Hoult was a bit more cosmopolitan; after all, he taught at a non-Jewish school. But I think he had little or no contact with his fellow-teachers outside of school.

And --- most important of all as far as Anne and I were concerned --- the Hoults expected their daughter to marry another Jew.

These were Anne's parents. They had become a part of British society; they were loyal British subjects and good, law-abiding citizens in every way. But the fear and mistrust of Gentiles was still strong. Their dearest wish, their most cherished ambition for their only daughter, was twofold: first, to see her graduate from University (I shall have more to say later, about the traditional Jewish veneration for learning); and second, to see her married to a nice Jewish boy, preferably a college graduate like herself --- best of all, a member of one of the liberal professions, doctor, lawyer, dentist. Actually, Anne's mother's first priority would be to see her married to the Nice Jewish Boy; to have her graduate from University was more her father's pet dream. For these things to happen would be a sort of vindication --- not only of their own lives, but of those of their ancestors, who for centuries had struggled for survival in a hostile, often cruel, society, and finally, after great travail, made good their escape to what they hoped would be a better one. The Hoult's dream for Anne had no place in it for me. This, essentially, was what Anne meant when she said to me: "There's no future for us two."

But I was not about to let myself be easily discouraged.

Anne's reason for rejecting my suit was quite incomprehensible to me, and I refused to accept it. I have tried to explain it above, in a few words. Even after you have read my attempt at explanation, it may still be difficult to understand, if the background is not familiar to you. It all seems pretty clear to me, now; but I've had fifty years since then, in which to find out what it was all about. At that time, I couldn't make head or tail of it. It seemed reasonable enough that she might expect *me* to object to her being Jewish (in my world, after all, that was anything but a mark of social eligibility); but since I didn't, what possible obstacle could be in our way? My family? I'd already considered that eventuality, and dismissed it.   My family were far away; and if they didn't fancy my choice, too bad; that wouldn't be reason enough for me to change it.   And she did not conceal from me the fact that I myself, personally, "found favour in her eyes," as the Bible puts it. So what **was** the matter, then? **Her** family? They hadn't even seen me yet. Why was she so certain of their disapproval that she wouldn't let me meet them --- hadn't yet dared let them know that I existed, even? In my utter ignorance, I was wholly at a loss to understand why Anne should turn me down.

Seeing that I wasn't going to let her reject me on those terms, Anne tried another tack.

"I shan't be staying in England after I graduate."

Why not? Where was she going?

"I'm going to Israel."

Israel? I wasn't even sure I knew exactly where it was.   Altogether, I knew very little about it; I thought that until quite recently it had been called Palestine, and located somewhere out East. As for what was going on there --- I was as uninformed about such things as the average Englishman; if possible, perhaps even less informed.   Current events have never been my strong point; and since my arrival in England, I'd been too preoccupied with the immediate events of my own life to take much interest in contemporary history --- *What on earth was she going there for?*

"To help build up a homeland there, for my people."

This was an easy one to counter, and I did so without hesitation --- *Well, couldn't I come along, too, and help?*

It was a lucky thing, really (for me --- not necessarily for Anne), that I was so abysmally ignorant. If I'd had even the faintest idea of what we were talking about, I might have hesitated, faltered, got cold feet, had second thoughts --- might have accepted Anne's dictum that there was no possible future for the two of us together, and regretfully agreed to give up on our relationship and seek a life partner elsewhere. Then my life would have been very different --- and I probably wouldn't have ended up writing about it.

But in a combination of utter ignorance and passionate desperation (have I made it clear how desperately I was in love with Anne?) I had no doubts at all. --- So why couldn't I come along and help build up a homeland for Anne's people, if that was what she wanted to do?

This was an option that Anne hadn't considered, and she had no ready reply. I pressed my advantage. I had no plans for the future. England had no special attractions for me; neither had Chile. I had already broken my childhood ties with my family, when I came to England. They weren't really expecting me back. Hardly any of the men in my family, for the past two or three generations, had spent their lives in the country of their birth. Going to Israel with Anne seemed just as feasible to me as any other future. And it had that one inestimable advantage over any other prospect: it had Anne. If she'd told me that she planned to go to the Kurile Islands, to help build up a homeland for the Hairy Ainu, I'd probably have demanded to tag along there, too.

She didn't refuse my suggestion outright. She said she'd think about it. On the one hand, the idea had for her its positive aspects. Foremost of these --- it would keep us together. By this time I wasn't the only one in love. Anne's feelings for me had become stronger than she had so far allowed herself to admit. Otherwise I would already have been sent packing, before things got so thoroughly out of hand.

The potential obstacles, on the other hand, were formidable.   First there were Anne's parents. Could their opposition be overcome? Opposition there would be, no doubt of that; probably very strong, too. Anne was an intelligent and perceptive girl, but her feelings were clouding her judgment, and it is possible that she herself didn't fully realize just how strong the opposition would be --- from her mother in particular. Anne herself had become "assimilated" enough to be able to consider me seriously as a life partner; but her parents were a generation behind.   Then there was the larger background to consider, apart from her parents. There were Anne's friends. Most of these were, like her, active in a Zionist youth movement dedicated to the ideal of building up a Jewish national home in Israel. What would they think of letting in an outsider like myself? And even if they were willing to take me on --- how about the organization to which they belonged? Would I be acceptable to the powers that be?

Did the State of Israel have any interest in a person like me? I still had only the barest notion of what any of these questions might mean. Anne had a much clearer idea of how difficult things might become.   Nevertheless, she said "We'll see what happens," and went off to consult her friends.

~~~~~~~~~~~~~~~~~~~~~~~~~~

Within a few days I was introduced to Joan, a pretty, vivacious young woman who was Anne's best friend, to be given the once-over. I suppose I passed muster; for a few days later, Anne took me to the clubhouse where her Zionist youth club held its activities. It was a large house of three or four stories in a well-to-do residential area, and was the property of the Zionist Federation of Great Britain. There seemed to be a lot of activity. Anne told me there were several hundred members, boys and girls aged mostly between about ten and twenty.

There I met the group among whom were Anne's closest associates and friends --- Brenda, Joyce, Harold, Malcolm, Irene, Moshe. Remembering them, I am suddenly, forcibly struck by the realization that that was more than half a century ago. The owners of those young, smiling faces are today elderly people like myself. Some of them are dead. A number of them live in Israel, and are my friends still.

The initial feeling of strangeness wore off very quickly. Anne's friends appeared willing to accept me on her say-so; they were cheerful, pleasant, asked me very few questions, and were at pains to make me feel welcome.

I met Gerald, the club director. He was a few years older than the rest. He had been assigned to the job by youth movement headquarters in London; after a tour of duty lasting a year or two, he would rejoin the settlement group to which he belonged, and they would travel together to Israel to begin a new life as pioneers, in a *kibbutz*. Gerald, too, was friendly and helpful. Anne had already briefed him about me. --- So I was interested in joining Anne in building up the Jewish homeland in Israel? Very well, why didn't I come along with her to a meeting or two, and learn a little more about it?

From the first moment I was made to feel at ease. Nobody made a big fuss of me. You might have thought this sort of thing happened every day. For all I knew, it *was* happening every day (since then I have learned that, if not exactly an everyday occurrence, my case is not unique --- lots of non-Jews like me have arrived in Israel; some have stories far more improbable than mine). I began accompanying Anne to meetings, and paid close attention to everything that went on, while keeping as low a profile as possible.

I learned that the club was part of a world-wide organization, a Zionist youth movement called *"Habonim"* (a Hebrew word meaning "The Builders"). Its objective: to encourage and educate its members to emigrate to Israel, and to settle there on the land, as pioneers. The form of settlement advocated by this particular youth movement was called "*kibbutz*": a sort of Utopian socialist agricultural collective, in which property was held in common by all members. I learned that there were already hundreds of such settlements in Israel, adding up to tens of thousands of members. The first of them, Deganiah, had been founded as far back as 1910.

All this was completely new to me. At that time, not too many people in the western world had heard of *kibbutz*. Ironically, nowadays many people are familiar with the name, and most of them will have at least some idea of what it means. I say "ironically" because today, the future of the *kibbutz* in Israel does not look nearly as secure as it did then. There are many more *kibbutzim* today than there were fifty years ago, and their total population is numbered in hundreds, not tens, of thousands; yet many of their members are clamouring to dismantle the socialist framework entirely --- to "privatize," and revert to traditional bourgeois modes of social and economic organization. A number of *kibbutzim* are already well down the road to achieving this. Many of the advocates of this revolution (or counter-revolution?) are the younger members, some of them the second or third generation born on *kibbutzim*.

In *Habonim* in 1949, though, "*kibbutz*" was a word to conjure with. The senior members of the movement, like Anne, would say it in tones of wonder and a little awe. They were very sincere in their pioneering ideals. There is ample testimony to this idealism to be found in Israel today: thousands of graduates of *Habonim*, and their descendants, live here --- many of them in *kibbutz*im, others in towns and villages the length and breadth of the country. That this is so, says a lot for the dedication and commitment of the young people who ran *Habonim*, acting as its organizers, administrators, and youth leaders.

The activities of these young people were regarded with a degree of ambivalence by their parents, and by the older generation in general. The Jewish community of Great Britain at that time was overwhelmingly "middle class," and committed to middle class values and ideals (I think Anne's parents were pretty typical). The idea of their children going to Israel and becoming farm labourers *("well, a kibbutz is a farm, isn't it? and you're going to work on it, aren't you? well, then!")* did not at all appeal to most of them. On the other hand, those were exciting days for the Jewish community: a Jewish State had appeared on the map, and was fighting for its life, and needed all the support it could get. Nobody could be against that. So Jewish parents all over the country allowed their children to join *Habonim*, without necessarily espousing all the ideas it stood for. Many of them believed, I think, that as their kids grew older, they would eventually come to their senses, and let someone else's children go to Israel and dig potatoes and fight Arabs.

Though the ideas and ideals behind *Habonim* may not have appealed to Anne's parents, they were very palatable to me. They had been dreamed up, after all, by idealistic young people; and they were taught in the youth movement in a manner designed to make them attractive to other young people. Socialism. Sharing. Brotherhood. *"From each according to his ability --- to each according to his needs."* Building a new home upon the ruins of the past.   Making the desert blossom like a rose.......... This is heady stuff, especially for a young person. It went to *my* head, at any rate, in no time at all.

There was an "underdog" side to the story, too, to make it even more appealing. I remember one day Anne and I were looking together at a map of the world. She pointed with her pencil to Israel's location. The pencil point pretty well blotted out the entire country. "That's us," she said. Then she swept her pencil round the whole Middle East. "That's what *they've* got," she said. "There are more than two hundred million of them," she went on, "and less than two million of us in Israel --- maybe twenty million in the whole world."

Anne was an enthusiastic guide for me into this fascinating and surprisingly congenial new world. As time went on I became more and more interested, and more and more involved.

~~~~~~~~~~~~~~~~~~~~~~~~~

Now we both had to let our families know what we proposed to do.

I didn't anticipate much of a hullabaloo from my family. Many people have a hard time with "parental expectations": their parents cherish all sorts of ambitions and hopes for them --- things like becoming a successful engineer, or taking over

Daddy's interior decorating business, or being world chess champion. Quite often, these expectations have mostly to do with the unfulfilled dreams of the parents themselves, and bear little relation to the needs or desires of the children.

My parents were very liberal in this respect. So long as my brothers and I did nothing dishonorable, they pretty well left us to choose our own futures, and did all they could to help us. "We want you to be happy. If that's what it takes --- go ahead." When I wrote and told my parents what I was up to, their response showed little of the bewilderment they must have felt.

From what I've already told you about my family, it must be clear that the last few generations weren't a particularly stay-at-home lot. There's lots more I didn't tell --- about my father's elder brother Charlie, for instance, who left home (in Birkenhead) in his teens, to look for silver and gold in the Andes, returning home only to enlist at the outbreak of World War One (he died at the Battle of the Somme, along with a million other men, fighting To Save Civilization For King And Country). Nonetheless, I think my choice of a purpose in life struck my parents as being a bit *outré*, even for a family like ours. But whatever they thought or felt, they took it bravely. Auntie

Ethel took her cue from them. She asked me if my parents knew what I was up to, and once satisfied that they did, she made no fuss.

Anne had it tougher. What *she* had to do was to inform her parents that one of their worst nightmares had come to pass. She spared me a lot of the details, but I think it must have been pretty awful. Her father, once he understood that Anne and I were in earnest, did his best to reconcile himself to the situation. He loved Anne dearly, and had no intention of giving her up. Which was just as well; for I think Mrs. Hoult would quite probably have turned Anne out, if she'd had her way. Mrs. Hoult was not a particularly happy woman; I think that at the best of times, her life was full of all sorts of dissatisfactions. And now here was Anne, coming with a piece of news which would poison her life entirely. It would wreck Mrs. Hoult's social standing with the ladies of her circle, at the synagogue, at her "Daughters of Zion" meetings. People would look at her knowingly, with sidelong glances, and talk behind her back about her misfortune, her daughter's disgrace. Her friends would regard her with pity --- her enemies, with malicious glee.

Anne once told me a story, which may help to put what I am telling in clearer perspective, in case you find it hard to understand.   It concerned her uncle Jack, her father's elder brother.   For reasons unknown to Anne, Jack decided in his youth to turn his back entirely on his Jewish identity.   He changed his name to a non-Jewish-sounding one (like Hoult), moved to a city where he was not known, and married a Christian Englishwoman. Their two daughters were brought up as Christians, with no knowledge (until adulthood, at any rate) of their Jewish parentage; one of them, Anne told me, became a Christian missionary in foreign parts (and didn't like Jews, said Anne, one little bit).   Anne learned the story from her father, who was privy to his brother's doing --- unlike *their* father, Anne's grandfather, a practicing Orthodox Jew, who was never allowed to know the truth.

Being a dutiful son, Jack continued to visit his father periodically throughout the latter's life, always alone (heaven knows what story he made up to account for this).   If her grandfather had known what Jack had done, said Anne, he would not only have refused to see him ever again; he would have torn his clothes, and gone into mourning for a son who was dead.   When I first heard this story, it struck me as pretty far-fetched; today, I know it isn't at all.   Jewish religious law forbids a Jew to marry outside the community, and calls for expulsion of the offender. Observant Jews take this prohibition very seriously. This has nothing to do with the personal qualities of the individuals concerned; it is simply an absolute prohibition against intermarriage with people of other faiths.

If you ever saw a musical called "Fiddler on the Roof," you may remember what a calamity it was for Tevye the milkman, when his daughter got involved with a Russian youth.

Anyway --- the cat was out of the bag at last.

Oddly enough, I don't remember the first occasion when I met Anne's parents. My life was so crowded with new experiences at that time, that I suppose I can't expect to remember them all; yet I should have thought that this particular event would have stayed with me. Still. Whatever happened on that occasion, it can't have been fun. There was nothing to be done about the way Anne's mother felt about me. This had nothing to do with me as a person. It was what I *stood for* that she couldn't bear: the ruination of all her hopes.

Anne's father, on the other hand, once he'd decided that they were stuck with me for better or for worse, did what he could to ensure that things were better rather than worse. He and I eventually became quite good friends. He was a small, slight man, with greying hair, and very bright, myopic eyes (like Anne's) behind his spectacles. He taught at a State school. To be less conspicuous in a mostly non-Jewish milieu, he had changed his name from Israel Hirschberg to Ellis Hoult. His wife still called him "Izzy" at home. He was a keen, lively, and well-informed conversationalist; we spent many hours talking.

He suffered from chronic constipation, which had become something of an obsession with him. He had a whole cupboard full of remedies for it, and was constantly trying new ones. Once he had got me marked down as a polite and patient listener (he was Anne's father; what else could I be?), I was subjected to regular, lengthy, bowel movement updates. I remember arriving one day at the Hoults' home, to be greeted by Mr. Hoult waving a medicine-bottle and crying happily: "Slippery Elm! Slippery Elm! I think I've found it at last!" He might have been a Knight of the Round Table, who had just stumbled unexpectedly upon the Holy Grail.

But he was a good man, who wanted to make things as easy as possible for Anne and me. Later on in our acquaintance, he raised the suggestion that I might consider getting converted to Judaism. Now, I wish I had (more about that later). But I didn't. I had no more objection to Judaism, as a religion, than I had to any other religion, including the one in which I was baptized; but as a freethinker, I thought it would be dishonest, and hypocritical, to go through the motions of making a covenant with a God I didn't believe in. I still think it would have been dishonest; the difference is that now, I have very good reasons for wishing I'd heeded Mr. Hoult's suggestion.

Anne and I no longer had to lead such hole-and-corner lives, now that our families knew about us, and there seemed to be no immediate problems with my acceptance into the youth movement. We spent more and more time together outside class hours, some of it at *Habonim*, some of it just doing the things all young people do. In the winter vacation we got ourselves jobs at Dunlop's rubber factory in Speke, outside Liverpool. Anne worked in the packing department, I in shipping. For both of us it was an eye-opening experience which we thoroughly enjoyed.

Neither of us had had very much contact with "working people" in our lives. I, in particular, had a lot of preconceived notions to overcome. My brothers and I had grown up in a society where class divisions were very deep. Our mother (much more so than our father) had a strong sense of belonging to a privileged class. This found expression in our being permitted to associate only with children whom our mother considered to be our social equals. What we were led to believe was that "poor people" were, if not actually dangerous, definitely not to be trusted, and certainly to be kept at a distance. The only contact you had with such people was when they worked for you, as domestic servants, labourers, etc.; in such cases, a degree of trust and even affection might develop in an individual relationship, but the social gulf remained. I remember our housemaids in Chile addressing my brothers and myself as "Don," "Don Elliott," even when we were quite small boys. And in England things weren't all that different. At the priests' school Larry and I attended before World War II, there was a boy named Harris. I can remember one of my friends whispering to me in confidence that Harris had been to a Council School. I'd no idea what a Council School was (I'm not really sure even now), but I recall the information made me feel a little uneasy. I steered clear of Harris from then on, as I would have done if I'd been told that his father was in prison, or that his mother was a charwoman.

Even after one has come to reject such attitudes on an intellectual level (I think I can truthfully say that by the time of which I am writing, I'd already made a start at doing that), they leave marks deep down in one's unconscious, which only experience can erase (if anything can). Working for a couple of weeks at the Dunlop plant was an intensive learning experience. The men in the shipping department knew what I was ("a college feller"), but didn't hold this against me. They taught me the skills of the work they did: I was eventually able to roll five automobile tires simultaneously, across the shipping room floor, around a corner, and on to the back of a lorry in the loading bay (you'll never know how much expertise this calls for, until you try doing it). They were patient with my ineptitude, and took pleasure in my progress. Their work was physically hard, intrinsically boring, and poorly paid, and they knew that it was what they would almost certainly be doing all their lives; yet they did it without bitterness, and sought their satisfactions elsewhere, outside of working hours. If they felt any resentment or anger about their way of life, they certainly didn't take it out on me: the worst I ever endured from them was a little good-natured chaffing on my clumsiness. They were kindness itself to me, and I for my part began to learn to admire and respect them.

Anne in the meantime had a great time with the girls (some of these "girls" were, in fact, middle-aged women) in the packing department. Here again, the work was boring, and badly paid; this did not keep these women from extracting every possible ounce of satisfaction, even fun, from their working day. There was a very strong camaraderie among them; their conversation reflected this --- they talked about the most intimate details of their lives, Anne told me, without the least reserve. Sex was a subject much discussed --- not a lot of theory; more of a daily update on any interesting experiences of the past twenty-four hours (*"Did you 'ave it last night, then, luv? Did yer coom? 'Ow many times, then?"*).

Information on birth control and abortion was eagerly shared. In Britain at that time, there was a very strong stigma attached to single motherhood, which cut across all social class divisions; some families would still turn a pregnant and unmarried girl out of the house. The Family Planning Association had clinics all over Britain, but most single girls would not want to be seen attending them. Popular methods of birth control did not seem to have changed much since Dr. Marie Stopes' stark description of them thirty years earlier, and appeared to be limited chiefly to *coitus interruptus* and abortion.

Since abortion was illegal in Britain at that time, the services of a skilled abortionist were beyond the reach of any but the wealthy, who would usually travel abroad to obtain them (my source for this kind of information was Uncle Richard, a doctor).   Among working girls, do-it-yourself abortion was the rule. Some of the methods used were pretty desperate, and occasionally fatal. One method which particularly interested Anne and me, because of its biochemical nature, involved taking (simultaneously) massive doses of Beecham's Pills (a laxative) and copious quantities of gin. What these two products have in common, we figured out, is extract of juniper, which apparently induces contraction of smooth muscle. Sitting in a hot mustard bath (presumably, to produce an irritation in that part of the body) while taking this "treatment," was believed to increase the chances of success.

All this stuff was of more than merely academic interest to Anne and me, for we had become lovers. Anne was terrified of getting pregnant; every month she welcomed the advent of her periods (which were very painful) with relief amounting almost to joy. In fact, the opportunities we had for getting her pregnant were few and fleeting; but the fear was ever-present --- almost obsessive. In retrospect, I am amazed at the courage and devotion she showed in even letting me get near her.

As my involvement with the activities of Anne's youth movement became greater, so I had less and less time for other things. I gave up my association with the rowing club. I was too busy with my new life, fortunately, to regret this at the time. Now I can look back, and see clearly how much that rowing club did to make my life easier during a difficult period. I had happy times there, and cherish the memory of them.

The months went by, and examination time came round. Anne and I passed all our examinations --- without too much difficulty, but without distinction either. We had far too many things distracting us, to make a good academic showing. In the summer I found myself a job as a labourer on a building site at Arrowe Park, not far from Wallasey. Once again I had first-hand contact with "working people," and an opportunity to reassess many of the social values I had been taught, and to form my own ideas. I stayed on that job during much of the summer vacation --- almost two months. I was learning as much outside the University classrooms as inside them.

Not long after the beginning of my third year of studies, I left Auntie Beatrice's home, and went into lodgings in Liverpool. We both thought it would be a good idea. She had faithfully discharged her undertaking to look after me --- had it not been for her steadying influence, I doubt if I'd ever have made it into second year at University --- and needed a rest; and I, for my part, welcomed the freedom of action which the move would give me. Once she was relieved of responsibility for me, our relations improved. I eventually came to see her as the good, brave woman she was, and I think she became fond of me, too.

After I'd been living in lodgings for a few weeks, I received an offer from Gerald, the director of the *Habonim* youth club. He had just got married, and his bride, Sylvia, was coming to live with him in the clubhouse, to act as a sort of housemother. It was a big house, said Gerald, with several empty rooms on the top story. I could have one of these for bedroom and study. Sylvia would take care of my domestic needs --- food, laundry, etc. --- and I would pay her the same as I was paying my present landlady (I think it was about three pounds a week).

I accepted, and moved in. Another young man of my age, Frank, moved in on the same terms, at about the same time. Frank was studying to be an optometrist. He and I got along well. We used to play table-tennis with furious intensity for hour after hour. The four of us lived together in the clubhouse for the rest of the year, until I graduated. Sylvia took good care of us all. With this arrangement, I became even more totally immersed in the activities of *Habonim*. I began to attend Hebrew classes. I helped Anne to prepare educational material --- posters and such (she was a talented draughtswoman and artist). Gerald suggested I might try my hand at leading one of the youth groups. I declined; I didn't feel qualified. I still felt very much of a newcomer; my education --- in Zionist and Socialist theory, Jewish history, Hebrew language, Middle East politics, you name it --- was proceeding apace, but I knew I was only scratching the surface. This was a whole new world, and I had still a great deal to learn about it. It's funny --- over fifty years have passed since then, and I think I've managed to learn a good deal; yet things keep happening almost every day, to remind me how much I have still to learn...........

One incident that I recall, which occurred early on in our relationship, may help to give you an idea of how ignorant I was of the world that Anne lived in, and how different it was, below the surface, from mine. One day she and I were strolling along a street in Liverpool, and we noticed that many of the businesses had Jewish names: "Dr. F. Spector --- General Practitioner"; "Abraham Goldberg, Gents' Tailoring," and such. Anne turned to me, smiling. "D'you know, Chil," she said, "It's so good to see all these Jewish names. It makes me feel sort of comfortable and at home, in a very special way." "Why's that?" I replied. "Is it because the Jews are God's chosen people?" She was horrified. A blow in the face would have shocked and hurt her much less. I think that what made me return such a brutally offensive answer may have been pique at her words (Why should she feel more comfortable surrounded by Jews than by Gentiles? What was wrong with the company of Gentiles, to make her feel uneasy? *I* was a Gentile, after all --- did *my* company make her feel that way?).

I still hadn't really got the picture, you see. What Anne was telling me was that the only people among whom she felt completely safe from racist provocation or harm, were other Jews like herself. And by telling me this, she was by implication "counting me in." But I still had to learn that a Jew who has grown up surrounded by Gentiles, even in the most tolerant and pluralistic of societies, is always to some extent on guard --- waiting for the snide remark, the sneer, the slur, the reminder that he, or she, is not quite the same as the others. This doesn't apply only to a Jew, of course, but to any member of a disadvantaged minority, anywhere. Israel Arabs, living among Jews, are in the same predicament.   My friend Saïd Khatib put it succinctly once, after a nasty racial incident at work. "Being in a minority is *harra* (shit)," he said.

On that street in Liverpool I failed Anne miserably, and vindicated her mother's worst fears.   Anne didn't give up on me there and then. But I hurt her very badly.   Ignorance is the only plea I can enter in mitigation of my crassness.   I wonder just what doubts may have crossed her mind, about the wisdom of the course that she was undertaking with me.   In any event --- she forgave me.

~~~~~~~~~~~~~~~~~~~~~~~~

My third year of study was almost up.   I had no interest in staying on at University (to get an Honours degree, I should have had to continue studying for another year); I was keen to get on with the next stage of my new life.   This had already been worked out between Anne, myself,

Gerald, and the powers that be at *Habonim* headquarters in London. After graduating, I would go to one of the training farms maintained in England by the *Habonim* youth movement, in cooperation with the Zionist Federation of Great Britain. There I would join a group of young people who were already preparing themselves for a pioneering life in Israel. Anne could not come with me; she was required to complete a minimum three years of study, in order to get her degree. She would join me the following year, and after our training period was over, we would travel to Israel together.

My parents arrived in England on a visit. Their purpose was several-fold (what they didn't tell me, I knew them well enough to figure out for myself): they wanted to meet Anne and her parents, and find out more about what I was getting myself into (they still cherished a hope that I might be open to dissuasion); they were bringing Ronald with them, to start the next stage of *his* education; they wanted to visit other members of our family who were living in England; they wanted to attend my graduation ceremony; they had itchy feet and felt like doing some travelling, and this was a good occasion. So they had plenty of reasons for coming. They travelled (as most people still did in those days) by ship. I met them at the dock, and saw them settled comfortably into the lodgings I had arranged for them.

They met Anne and her parents. If there was any embarrassment, it was probably on the Hoults' side. My parents were unaware of most of the deeper undercurrents in the relationship between Anne and myself, which I have tried to describe in the last few chapters. They were quite ready to have her as daughter-in-law. It was our plans for our future together which had them puzzled and worried.

Altogether, things didn't go too badly. My mother had an engagement ring made up for Anne, with diamonds from a bracelet she'd once been given by her father, in our family's palmy days. Ronald had decided to join the British Army for a few years. In the Royal Electrical and Mechanical Engineers (REME) he expected to gain additional experience in his chosen profession. It was a wise move. During the five years he spent in REME he acquired a first-class education as a master mechanic --- and in addition, had a whale of a time, most of it in Malaysia, Singapore, and other places in South-East Asia.

My parents were very good about the subject of my future.   Any attempts to dissuade me from my chosen course of action were very soft-pedal.   My father asked me if I was still interested in changing over from Science to Medicine (there'd been some tentative talk of this a year earlier, but it had come to nothing); if I were, he said, he'd be willing to foot the bill for the next four or five years ---- however long it took.   I declined with thanks; I was already marching to the sound of a different drum.   After a while they dropped the subject.

Graduation day came.   I received my degree: "Ordinary Degree of B.Sc., Class II."   There was one degree lower: Class III.   I think if you sank as low as that, suicide was more or less expected of you. Never mind, it was good enough to land me a job, later, when I needed one.   And I've met lots of people in Israel and elsewhere, with all sorts of degrees high and low, who I don't believe could have made that Class III, even if they'd spent a lifetime trying.   The academic garb (rented for the ceremony) was very smart: black gown, with black hood, trimmed with ermine and lined with peacock-blue silk.

Underneath the gown, I wore mostly borrowed finery: the suit, shirt, and tie were Mr.   Hoult's; only the socks, the underwear, and I *think* the shoes, were all mine. My parents were happy; most of all, relieved, I think, that I'd at least made it this far. I was glad too: at any rate, they'd had that much satisfaction from me. Anne had a terrible disappointment: she wasn't accepted for the Honours School. This meant that after her mandatory third year of study, she would only get an Ordinary degree like mine, and would have to study for a fourth year if she wanted to get an Honours degree. Our love affair had taken its toll of her studies, as well as of mine.

Very soon after graduation, I embarked on a new venture. I travelled South to The Grange, near Twyford in Berkshire. The Grange was a big farmhouse, built in the 1880's by some wealthy townsman who could afford to lose money playing gentleman farmer. It had about 45 acres of farm land, and was now owned by the Zionist Federation of Great Britain. It was on loan to the *Habonim* youth movement, who used it for the last stage of training for pioneers, before their emigration to Israel. About 20 or 25 young people lived there as a commune. Most of them worked as labourers for farmers round about (a farm labourer's pay was so meagre, and the work so hard, that it was almost always possible for any inexperienced young man or woman to get some sort of job in agriculture); a handful worked on the home farm and in the house. All income was pooled, all expenses shared. The idea was to help prospective pioneers make the transition from pampered middle-class city-dwellers to hard-working socialist farmers, before arriving in Israel. The normal training period was two years.

I did not join the commune straightaway; I was coming to The Grange to take part in a session of the *Habonim Institute*. This was a sort of high-octane indoctrination course, aimed primarily at Jewish university students. It was intended to raise the level of Zionist and Socialist awareness among the participants, through six weeks of intensive study and discussion. There were about forty young men and women taking part. We were lodged in makeshift quarters in the barns and outbuildings of the farm. During the day we studied and discussed; in the evenings we mingled with the members of the commune after their day's work, and argued interminably about every subject under the sun. I spent a very stimulating six weeks at the *Habonim Institute*. The chief instructors were high-powered intellectuals: one of them went on to become Professor of Semitic Studies at Cambridge University; another ended up many years later as Israel's first ambassador to the

People's Republic of China. I think most of the participants had a wonderful time; I know I did.

My parents concluded their visit to Britain and went back to Chile. Ronald joined the British Army. Anne went back to University. I joined the commune.

3. Zionism and life at The Grange

I became wholly absorbed into life in the commune at The Grange. We didn't refer to ourselves as a commune: we called ourselves a "*Kibbutz Hachsharah.*" "*Hachsharah*" is a Hebrew word meaning "preparation" or "making ready" for something. We were making ourselves ready for a life as pioneers in Israel. There were about 25 of us, with three or four more men than women. Our ages ranged between 18 and about 24. Two of us worked in housekeeping (food purchasing and preparation, cooking, cleaning, laundry, clothes repair, and general house upkeep); three more worked on the home farm; the rest of us worked outside.

We were usually able to find ourselves jobs within cycling range, that is, within a radius of six or seven miles around The Grange. We had a collection of ramshackle bicycles: these were maintained by the "Bike-man," an elected official whose duty was to keep them in working order, mend punctures for those who couldn't do their own repairs, see to the supply of lamps and batteries, etc. I don't know where the bikes came from; we never, to my knowledge, bought a new one while I was there. This was just as well --- discussions as to who should be the proper person to use it would have been interminable. I shall have more to say about discussions. They were a group activity of major importance.

This group was intended to eventually form what is known as a *garin*, which literally means in Hebrew a "seed." In other word we were the seed of a new settlement of a *kibbutz* in the Land of Israel. Everyone in the *garin* had a Hebrew name. Since my name was Elliott, everyone called me El, which was fine by me, since El was the name of God in the earliest part of the Bible. Later on I fixed on the Hebrew name *Ariel*.

Now I want to tell you in more detail about our communal life at The Grange, but I don't know what to put in and what to leave out. There's so much to tell. Perhaps the best way to begin is to say that never in my life, before or since that time, have I felt myself living with so strong a sense of purpose --- so **intensely**. I am not speaking of the physical regime we imposed upon ourselves --- which was punishingly hard --- but of a state of mind. It's not easy to describe. Think of an engine going flat out all the time. Think of a long-distance runner pushing himself beyond exhaustion. Think of soldiers in euphoria of battle, eager to win glory in a holy cause, whatever the cost. We were all of these. We lived in a perpetual state of collective exaltation, driven by the ideals which we had all embraced, and sustained by constant and vociferous mutual analysis and criticism. Those endless discussions began almost every evening, as soon as we were all home from work and showered and fed --- and went on late into the night.

Our day began early. We had an "early shift" rota. One of us would get up at 4:15 or 4:30 am, stoke the cooker, make tea and toast, and do wake-up rounds every 15 minutes till about 6 o'clock. Very few of us got up the first time we were called: some of us needed three, or even four, calls at 15-minute intervals.   We would write our wake-up instructions with chalk, on the stones of the alcove in the kitchen where our "*Aga*" cooking range stood. This was a huge, marvellous contraption upon which three or four of us could perch comfortably at once. On a winter evening it was the warmest place in the house. It was as much institution as artefact.

By 6:00 am most of us would be up and about, still half asleep for the most part, getting our thermos bottles filled with tea, picking up our sandwiches

(prepared   the previous day by the kitchen
personnel), and shuffling (in my own case at least,
"lurching" is probably the most accurate word) out
to the bike shed if we had an outside job to go to. A
farm worker's day began routinely at 7 am; some
of us had to leave the house by 6 or 6:15 to get to
work on time. Everyone took a turn at early shift,
regardless of whether they worked "inside" or
"outside."   The only person exempt was Mike, the
cowman.   This was because Mike had to get up
early seven days a week to milk the cows, of which
there were half-a-dozen on the home farm. All the
rest of us got a long lie-in on Sunday; Mike got
none.

Around 4:30 or 5:00 pm, the outside workers
would start rolling in from work. There would be
time to take a shower, and possibly even snatch a
few minutes' rest, before the evening meal. Again,
there was a rota (two at a time) for serving supper,
clearing away, and washing up (the actual
preparation of the meal was done earlier, by the
household staff.   But all such domestic jobs after
working hours, and at week-ends, were shared by
all of us on a rotating basis). Soon after supper, the
evening programme would begin.   There was
always an evening programme. This was a point of
principle. We were there preparing ourselves to

be pioneers. Our time had to be usefully occupied; an evening without a programme would be an evening thrown away (I didn't think all that much of this notion, but didn't try to contest it: it wouldn't have done any good. A principle was a principle).

The programs took various forms. Someone might come from the W.E.A. (Worker's Educational Authority) to give us a talk about bee-keeping, or rearing chickens. Occasionally the farm manager, Mr. White, would come and talk to us about budgets and farm economics. Once in a while some big wheel might come down from the London headquarters of *Habonim*, and brief us about what was going on in "the Movement," as we called it. Or we might hear a talk about Israel from a "*shaliah*" --- one of the emissaries sent to England from Israel by the *Kibbutz* organization with which *Habonim* was affiliated. If our evening's programme did not include anyone from outside, we would schedule meetings and discussions, in one or more of our innumerable committees.

We had committees for everything. The "housing committee" dealt with who shared a room with whom. This subject could be (and always was) discussed in depth: it offered endless opportunities for the minute public examination of personal traits and behaviour to which we constantly subjected each other. The "culture committee" dealt with the programming of intellectual activities outside of working hours. The "work committee" discussed people's jobs. Who should work in the house; who should work on the home farm; who should work outside?

Farm jobs were more difficult to find in winter; was it all right for Elliott to get work as a builder's labourer? (The answer: yes. Almost any job was better than none at all). The "members' committee" dealt with personal matters of individual members. Just about any aspect of a member's behaviour could be (and was) discussed and criticized here.

We had technical committees, too, to discuss questions such as food, budgets, purchasing. What was the maximum cigarette ration which we could allow ourselves? Our answer: 35 Woodbines a week (a Woodbine was a wretchedly undersized mini-cigarette, favoured by working people of limited means), or one ounce (28 g) of cigarette tobacco to roll your own. We used a lot of cigarette papers: with practice, you could roll 60 matchstick-thin cigarettes from an ounce of tobacco. Also, "dog-ends" --- cigarette butts --- could be saved and re-rolled. About five dog-ends made one additional smoke (......and yet *another* dog-end. Recycling buffs would have loved us).

Should non-smokers get an extra allowance of sweets "in lieu?" Our answer: no. Our official ideological rationale was that smoking was a legitimate need, whereas candy was a luxury. If you didn't *need* tobacco, there was no reason for you to be given something else instead. Smokers or not, we all got the same allowance of candy: four ounces (113.5 grams) a week. It was usual to take one's allowance in sweets that went a long way: Rowntree's Fruit Gums were a favourite. In a fit of contrariness, I remember taking my ration for a time in sugared almonds. It amounted to about five or six almonds in all. They tasted great.

We had almost as many committees as we had members, so nobody was exempt from duty on at least two or three committees. Most committee deliberations resulted in recommendations, to be brought before a general meeting of all members. All decisions of importance were made at general meetings, of which we had at least one or two a week. Once a year at election time, when all the committees were re-staffed, and new officers (secretary, treasurer, "bike-man," etc.) chosen, we would have several general meetings a week, for weeks on end. At these meetings we could re-hash, and expand on *ad aeternam*, the arguments already raised and discussed in committee. All of us attended all meetings. Non-attendance was simply not countenanced: the only acceptable reasons for not being at a general meeting were physical absence from the *kibbutz*, or serious illness.

~~~~~~~~~~~~~~~~~~~~~~~~

At week-ends the pace of our activity continued almost unabated, but the content changed somewhat, beginning with Friday night. The hours between getting back from work on Friday afternoon, and sitting down to supper on Friday evening, were among the most hectic of the week: for on Friday evening occurred what was, in a cultural sense, perhaps the week's most important event: the *Kabbalat Shabbat,* or welcoming of the Sabbath.

The fourth of the Ten Commandments is "Remember the Sabbath Day, to keep it holy." It ranks in order of primacy above those commandments which forbid murder, adultery, theft, perjury, and covetousness; even above the commandment to honour one's father and mother. A recognition of the special difference between the Sabbath (*Shabbat*) and the remaining days of the week (*yemei hol*: profane days, as distinct from the holy day) is a central feature of Jewish national consciousness, no matter how far removed a Jew may be from religious observance of any kind. I have read of Christian families in Latin America, in which the mother lights two candles every Friday evening at dusk. If asked why she does this, she will reply that her mother did it before her. These people are from families whose Jewish ancestors in Spain or Portugal were forcibly baptized 500 years ago or more. They may be wholly unaware of ever having been Jewish, and yet retain this vestige of Jewish ritual.

Habonim, the youth movement to which we all belonged, was a secular organization, predicated on principles of Socialist Zionism. You weren't required to believe in God to be a member, or to observe any Jewish religious commandments. In fact, you weren't required even to be a Jew, so long as you accepted the socialist-Zionist ideology (nobody in *Habonim* that I know of, ever had any problem accepting me. I was never set apart in any way). There existed other youth organizations, and other pioneer movements, for young Zionists who needed to express their Jewishness in actual religious ritual observance (such as keeping the Sabbath, conformance with Jewish dietary laws, etc.). There were --- and are --- religious *kibbutz*im in Israel, in which a religious-minded Jew could live in fulfilment of the ideals of Socialist Zionism, and at the same time remain fully committed to the requirements of Jewish religious practice.   This reflects the plurality of Zionist organizations worldwide, which have always sought to find common ground among Jews with a multiplicity of views about just what it means to be a Jew.   It has been said that there are as many different forms of Judaism as there are Jews in the world.   There is no supreme authority in Judaism, no Pope or Archimandrite or Council of Elders, with the absolute last word in laying down the law for everybody.   Every Jew, ultimately, defines Judaism for himself.   It is important to grasp this point if you ever want to have any idea at all of what Jewish history is all about.

I've said that *Habonim* was a wholly secular, socialist Zionist organization.   The worship of God played no part in it.   On the other hand, Jewish ritual (the observances with which Jews remind themselves that they are Jews) was very important. Jewish religious holidays were reinterpreted in humanistic terms, compatible with socialist Zionist ideology.   Passover (*Pesach*), for instance, the ancient festival celebrating the deliverance of the Children of Israel from slavery in Egypt, was observed by us, both as a welcoming of Spring (appropriate to the farming way of life to which we were committed), and as a celebration of Jewish political emancipation and the establishment of a sovereign Jewish state.

We wrote our own Passover *Hagadah,* a new one every year. It was half paraphrase, half parody of the real thing. Everyone who could was expected to contribute something to it. Much of it was humorous, full of "inside" topical references and allusions, poking fun at ourselves, our way of life, our beliefs and ideals, our elders; no sacred cow was safe from our satire. We worked on it for many weeks in advance; when the manuscript was complete, it was typed on waxed paper sheets, to which decorative illustrations were added by hand with a metal stylus, and finally mimeographed.

During the last couple of weeks before Passover, we would even cut back on meetings and ideological discussions; preparations for the *Seder* took precedence over all else. Besides the production of the *Hagadah* itself, the dining-room had to be decorated, with huge coloured pictures of Passover themes covering the walls. In the kitchen, special traditional Passover goodies were prepared and baked, using *matza* meal (instead of flour), coconuts, sugared carrots, almonds; age-old recipes which have been used by Jewish cooks for century after century. I was fascinated by every detail. I was just beginning to discover the incredible richness of texture which Jewish culture has acquired, during more than three thousand years of continuous development.

Our *seder* company usually included several guests --- among them, inevitably, Mr. and Mrs. W., Louis' parents. Louis was one of our unattached bachelor members. His mother was a Big Wheel in many Zionist organizations, and took a maternal interest in our commune. She was a good woman, who did us many kindnesses. Her visits remain associated in my mind with an incredible temporary abundance of cigarettes. Louis was a heavy smoker who, like the rest of us, found it hard to make do with our meagre tobacco ration. It was ideologically unacceptable for his mother to bring cigarettes only for him; whatever she brought had to be shared out equally. So she would bring dozens and dozens of packets, enough to ensure that even after an equitable distribution, Louis had plenty of smokes for a while, at least.

Another regular guest at our Passover *seder* was Mr. Weiser, our farm manager. Mr Weiser was originally from Austria, where he had been a farmer during the 1920's and 1930's. On his farm he had employed young aspiring Zionist pioneers from the Austrian and German branches of Habonim. When the Nazis came to power he had managed, somehow, to get away to safety while that was still possible. We knew him as a somewhat irascible man, and a hard taskmaster. Mike, Frank, and anyone else who worked on the home farm, were bossed around loudly and unrelentingly. We called him "Mr. Weiser" to his face, and "Charlie" behind his back. In our "Zigs" (humorous sketches which we made up and performed for every occasion) we constantly made fun of his Teutonic accent, and of his inventiveness at mispronouncing English farming terms. It was at our *Seder* in the spring of 1951 that an incident occurred involving Mr. Weiser --- a small thing, maybe, yet I shall remember it as long as I live.

It had to do with the J.N.F. tree certificates. The J.N.F. (Jewish National Fund) was established about 100 years ago by the World Zionist Organization, with the object of collecting money from Jews all round the world. The money would be used to buy land and equipment for aspiring pioneers, who wanted to settle in Palestine and till the soil, but lacked the wherewithal to do so. When I joined Habonim, just about every Jewish home in Britain (and in other countries around the world) had a familiar blue-and-white J.N.F. collecting box; a J.N.F. emissary would come round periodically and empty them. In 1948 the State of Israel was established, and anyone might have thought that the J.N.F.'s usefulness had come to an end. That may very well have been so, but that was no reason for it to shut down; for by that time, the J.N.F. had developed a life and a momentum of its own, and like many such institutions, no longer really needed any objectives beyond its own self-perpetuation. It had become an important and powerful player in the vast game of power-bases and patronage that is Israeli politics. In such a situation, functions can always be found for an organization of this kind. The J.N.F. was in charge of planting trees on Israel's denuded hillsides, and caring for the forests thus created. By paying a certain sum, you could have a tree, or any number of trees, planted in a forest in Israel in the name of a person or group of your choice, and the nominee would receive an attractively decorated certificate, attesting the event.

That year, we had a few JNF tree certificates handy at Passover time, to be ceremoniously presented as tokens of appreciation to people like Louis' mother. This time, one of our intended guests cancelled their visit, and the day before Passover we found ourselves with a certificate for three trees and nobody to give it to. "Why not give 'em to Charlie?," someone suggested jocularly. We all laughed agreement; this seemed an oddly amusing thing to do. So on the night of our *Seder*, the certificates were duly handed out; and Van, the presenter, held up the last one, saying: ".........and three trees for Mr. Weiser." Mr. Weiser stood up to take his certificate, and opened his mouth to acknowledge it --- but no words came: he was choked with emotion, his shoulders shook, and tears were running down his cheeks. Our joke had misfired. This was no joke to him. I felt ashamed, and moved. Our casual, light-hearted gesture had quite unexpectedly touched something very deep inside Mr. Weiser, which we hadn't known was there. One never knows.

The same sort of arrangement had to be done for the Sabbath. This is the most important of Jewish festivals (with one exception, which is *Yom Kippur*, the Day of Atonement). Its connotations are, at bottom, entirely religious. It is the day upon which God rested from his labour of Creation, and for that reason, it is holy, and a Jew subject to God's law is commanded to rest too. It isn't easy to find secular interpretations for the concept of Sabbath; and yet it is impossible to ignore. In Israel, if you take a look, on a Friday afternoon, at any one of the most militantly anti-religious *kibbutz*im ---- there are those who are as doctrinaire in their atheism, as any ultra-Orthodox rabbi in his Judaism ---- you will find people making ready to observe the Sabbath: putting on clean holiday clothes, setting out festive food different from that which is eaten on weekday nights --- including the *Hallah*, the loaf of bread made in a special shape, and baked from a special enriched mix, eaten by Jews on the Sabbath since time immemorial --- you may even find a pair of candles burning in a prominent place in the *kibbutz* dining-room. So deeply is the concept of Sabbath ingrained into the heart of a Jew. There may be a million different forms of Sabbath observance, for as many individuals; yet all have ultimately a common function --- a statement of Jewish identity, reiterated every seven days.

At The Grange we celebrated the Sabbath with a meticulously regulated Friday evening ceremony. After returning home from work, washing and bathing, we put on our Sabbath clothes (white shirts for the men, white blouses for the women) and assembled in the dining room, where the long tables were laid, with white tablecloths over the workaday formica, and loaves of *Hallah* set out. We would sing Sabbath songs in our makeshift

Hebrew (often without a very clear idea of what the words meant) until the last comer arrived, and our company was complete. Then one of the women would light the candles, and one of us would recite the Sabbath blessing, which begins: "...and it was evening, and it was morning, the sixth day; and the heavens and the earth were finished......" and concludes with the sentence, "blessed art thou, O Lord our God, King of the Universe, who makest the Sabbath holy." Then we would break bread, and the first course of Friday night supper would be served. At The Grange, the first course consisted invariably of tomato soup. On one occasion, an enterprising *economit* (housekeeper) tried to give us something else. This *faux pas* caused such an uproar that it was never repeated --- at least, not during the time that I was there.

Once supper was over, we would repair to the "*Klali*" or common-room and wait for the *toranim* (those individuals on duty clearing away and washing-up) to finish and join us, then the evening programme would begin. On Friday evening, this took the form of an "*Oneg Shabbat*" --- literally, "Sabbath Delight" --- our version of an old Jewish custom, practiced in many communities: a sort of Friday evening social gathering. Each of us in turn had to prepare a Friday night program. It might be simply a few readings from different sources on a common theme, for which several of us might be recruited as readers. It could include an original sketch, or playlet or short story, by the evening's presenter. The readings might be accompanied by, or interspersed with appropriate musical selections played on our gramophone (we had a considerable collection of records, mostly classical). Whatever each of us gave was acceptable, so long as one did the best one could. If the group felt for any reason that they were being fobbed off with a lot less than the presenter was capable of, disapproval would be shown in no uncertain terms. This didn't happen often. After the *Oneg Shabbat* we would adjourn, and head for our beds, and one more night of not enough sleep.

Saturday was a working day for English farmers, though shorter than a weekday; and so it was for us too, Sabbath notwithstanding. Most of us would get home some time during early or mid-afternoon. We slacked off our pace a little at the week-end --- but not much. For one thing, there were a lot of domestic chores to be done. Meals had to be prepared, served, and cleared away every Saturday and Sunday for the whole company. A rota took care of this; given our small number, this meant that each of us would do several hours' work in the house, about one week-end in two. Then there were other activities. The Zionist Federation of Great Britain paid for a Hebrew teacher, who came every week-end to give us some hours of instruction in the Hebrew language. Hebrew lessons were not optional. None of our collective activities were optional. We all took part in everything. This was a rule to which we stuck very closely.

~~~~~~~~~~~~~~~~~~~~~~~~~

I got myself a job in the same way as everyone else at the commune: by cycling round the countryside until I found someone who thought they could use me. The farmer who gave me my first job had a herd of about 50 cows. They were milked by machine. My first assignment was to help Fred, the farmer's other hired labourer and right-hand man, to milk the cows. I was shown how to apply the machinery to the cow's udders. Fred also pointed out those cows who didn't like to be milked by machine, and were milked manually. I was to pass over these; Fred and the farmer would deal with them.

I'd never been near a cow in my life. The rear ends of fifty cows all looked identical to me. I took the pail of cleaning fluid for washing the cows' udders before applying the suction cups. It was a dilute solution of sodium hypochlorite in water, pleasantly warm to my fingers, which were stiff with the chill of an early autumn morning (I started work at half past six, after a 40-minute bike ride to work). After wiping off the udder with a rag, I turned the valve on the suction header, and applied the cups. The cow's flank was warm against my cheek and had a pleasant, animal smell. This was easy.......

As I bent to put the cups on the fourth or fifth cow, I was knocked flat on my face by a violent blow in the side. The cow had knocked me down, and proceeded to add half-a-dozen more kicks in quick succession, while the suction cups belched and gurgled unheeded on the floor beside me. By the time I had got out from under, with Fred's help, my shirt was hanging in tatters from a very sore back indeed. "I told you not to try and put 'em on *her*," said Fred.

The milking got done eventually (with not much assistance from me), and Fred took me to the stable for my next assignment. There was a horse standing in the corner. "Take the horse and cart" said Fred, pointing to some harness lying at one side, "and cut a load of kale for the cows." Seeing me pick up the harness rather gingerly, with two fingers, he added: "What's the matter, then?"

"It's got some shit on it," I said.

Fred looked at me for a second, his face inscrutable, then looked away. "Rm-m" he said. "You'll get used to that."

Under Fred's guidance, I soon picked up the rudiments of farm routine. Seeing that I was strong, willing and an attentive listener, he was prepared to make allowance for my ignorance, and instructed me patiently. He seemed glad of my company, and was willing to talk occasionally as we worked together. I learned that he was married, but childless, and had been a farm worker all his life, save for an interval of war service.

He seemed to spend most of his waking life at work; so far as I could gather, he had no recreational activities at all. I didn't see him take a day off while I worked there (which wasn't, admittedly, all that long).

I was busy one day with some job or other, when Fred came over. "Here," he said, thrusting something into my hand. I looked: it was half a crown. Fred said: "I took a load of manure up to Jenkins' farm, and they gave me five bob. That's your share." Five shillings was a generous tip --- about one-quarter of a day's pay for a farm labourer. I tried to refuse, but Fred would have none of it. Half the money was my share. Anything else would have been unthinkable to him.

Everything Fred did, all the time we were working together, was consistent with the action I have just described. There was a sort of natural integrity about him which you couldn't miss. I'm not just fantasizing this. I've no idea if Fred subscribed to any political or religious ideology --- we didn't know each other long enough for me to find out. But I do know, with absolute certainty, that if I were ever to find myself in a really tight corner, back to the wall and with very little chance of ever getting out, Fred would be the sort of person I should want to have alongside me. The battle of Waterloo wasn't won on the playing-fields of Eton. It was won by people like Fred.

I didn't last long on that first job. It was because of the pay. I hadn't negotiated a wage with the farmer at the time he took me on. After the first week, he put some money into my hand. "Here's your pay." Employers were required by law, in Britain at that time, to pay their workers weekly in

cash.   It was a fairly recent law, passed as a result
of the various methods ---"company store," that
sort of thing --- which many employers had
devised over the centuries, for cheating their
workers out of part of their pay.

When I got back to the commune, and handed the
money over to Frank, our treasurer, he asked me:
"How many hours did you work this week?"   I
made a calculation. It had been a long week. Frank
then explained to me that in the commune, we
were all (including myself) members of the
N.U.A.W., or National Union of Agricultural
Workers.   The Union had negotiated a national
standard rate of pay for its members (I don't know
exactly who had represented the employers), and
that was the rate at which we expected to be paid.
Our basic working week was 47 hours, if I
remember rightly; any additional hours, and
likewise work at week-ends, were to be paid for at
overtime rates.   The amount the farmer had given
me (about five pounds) was less than I was entitled
to, by some two pounds.

The following week I brought up this subject with
the farmer. He turned out to be less well-informed
about recent social developments than was Frank.
I insisted on my proper rate of pay, and soon found
myself once again cycling through the country

lanes of Berkshire, looking for a more enlightened employer.

I learned eventually that there were many farmers who didn't know, or didn't want to know, about the N.U.A.W., and about standard rates of pay for hours worked. Post-war Britain had a Socialist government, and industrial trade unions were very powerful; but the organization of labour in agriculture was relatively feeble. I don't know what proportion of farm workers were union members, and got paid union rates. I doubt if it was very high (though some of the farmers for whom I subsequently worked, adhered strictly to the terms of payment agreed with the N.U.A.W.). Things like strikes --- common enough at that time in industry --- were unthinkable in agriculture, where history didn't seem quite to have caught up with the present. In all N.U.A.W. communications and meetings, members were still referred to, and addressed each other, as "Brother" --- as in the days of the Tolpuddle Martyrs, 120 years earlier, when trade unions were secret societies, and belonging to one was a serious crime.

There were other archaic survivals, like the "tied cottage." A farmer might have several cottages on his land, which would be allocated to labourers working for him. These were considered valuable job perks, by workers who could usually afford to own nothing beyond their clothes and a few movable articles. They served as incentives to stay on the job; for a labourer who lost his employment, would of course lose his home as well. Alf, one of the members of our commune, told us a story in this connection. One of the labourers working for Alf's employer got ill and died. This man lived with his family in one of a group of seven cottages owned by the farmer, who, as soon as the man died, told his widow to clear out, as he needed the house for the worker who would replace the dead man.

The widow, with several children, was naturally in no hurry to go, and went about finding out what she could do to avoid leaving. Times had changed. No longer could she be served an eviction order and turned out bodily (this would still have been possible, only a dozen years earlier); tenants now had rights, and the law said she could stay.

The farmer did what he could to get rid of the widow. The only supply of fresh water for all the seven cottages was a single water tap in the yard. He forbade her to use it, and also forbade all the other tenants to give her water, on pain of being deprived of water in their turn. So she was obliged to walk half a mile or so, to fetch water from the nearest faucet that wasn't on the farm.   I don't doubt that this was preferable to being turned out of doors with the kids.

I never heard the end of this story; but it tells something about what farm labourers in Britain had to put up with.   And this was despite the fact that there was a desperate shortage of workers in British agriculture at that time.   During World War II, many men left work on the land, either to join the armed forces or to find better-paid jobs in war industries.   Many of them never came back to the farms.   After the war, German prisoners-of-war facing repatriation were offered the possibility of staying in Britain, on condition that they worked in agriculture.   I met several of these during my time at The Grange, a full five years after the war's end.

I don't know why agriculture in Britain should have remained so socially backward right into modern times.   I suppose it has something to do with the British people's reverence for traditions, even for thoroughly rotten ones like their class system.   The dispossession and ill-use of the working rural population by the power-wielding classes, is a British tradition harking back to the Middle Ages.   Over the past 600 years in Britain, title to land, and the right to the use and disposal of it, have passed more and more exclusively into the hands of a privileged class. Most of the farmers for whom I and my fellows at The Grange laboured, were themselves tenants, with no title to the land they tilled: they paid rent for it --- more often than not, to the bailiff of some absentee owner whom they might never see.

In any event, this situation --- however regrettable in terms of British social history --- worked very much to the advantage of myself and other aspiring pioneers, at The Grange and the handful of other similar training farms scattered across southern Britain. We rarely went without a job for long, despite the dubious qualifications with which we embarked on our farming careers.

Remarkably soon, I felt as much at home in a barnyard as if I'd been born in one. Fred's prediction proved true: I became thoroughly accustomed to the feel, odour, and even to the taste of animal dung. I can remember eating my sandwiches one spring day, perched on top of a layer of manure five feet deep, in a calf-pen I was helping to clear out. I didn't even bother climbing down to wash my hands. I was well on the way to learning that almost all *really* disgusting odours are not natural, but man-made ---- except for one:

the smell of dead and decomposing flesh, which is the same for all animals, including humans.

~~~~~~~~~~~~~~~~~~~~

A few weeks after I joined the *kibbutz* at The Grange, Anne sent word that she was coming down for a week-end visit.   We'd been there together before, at the time of the *Habonim* Institute, of which I've already spoken. My fellow-members of the commune knew about our relationship; several of them were from Liverpool, and were old friends of Anne's. For our convenience and comfort, they arranged for us to have a bedroom at our disposal for the week-end (normally, I shared a bedroom with another bachelor). I should have been thrilled at the prospect of spending a week-end with my lover, untrammelled by the sort of social restraints which had made our love-life in Liverpool so difficult.

But I was not thrilled. Instead, I was filled with foreboding. The news of Anne's impending visit compelled me to face the fact that my ardour had cooled.   Suddenly, I was not at all sure that I wanted to share my life with Anne, after all.   And in that case, I was going to have to tell her so --- the sooner the better, which meant on her forthcoming visit.

This is not an episode in my life of which I can speak with any pride or satisfaction. Yet it is too important for me to skip entirely; so I shall try and tell it as truthfully and as accurately as I can, though it does not reflect any credit on me.

Only a few months earlier I had been ready, in the name of love, to change the entire direction of my life. I had, in fact, taken all the necessary steps to do so. How could a passion so compelling have cooled so thoroughly in so short a space of time? I haven't a ready answer for this. Those who knew Anne and myself then, and witnessed the events I am writing of, may have had explanations of their own, more credible than anything I can come up with.

My feelings for Anne were genuine enough at the time. They may have been made more intense by the circumstances under which they were conceived. The terrible loneliness and isolation in which I was living when I met Anne; the fact that when we met, she was the only woman of my own age whom I knew well enough even to nod and say "hello" to; the realization, for the first time in my life, that I could be attractive enough to a woman for her actually to care about me --- all of these may have fanned the flames of passion to a greater heat than might have otherwise been the case, had my background been more normal, and myself less overwrought at the time.

The Grange changed everything for me, very quickly and very drastically. I was no longer lonely; I doubt if I've ever felt less lonely in my life. I found myself deeply involved in a society of which, not long before, I would hardly have dared even to dream: a society in which men and women associated freely, as comrades, as equal participants in a fellowship unlike anything I'd ever known. Looking at the women in our *kibbutz*, I saw *all* women, and my own relationship to them, with different eyes.   And inevitably, I saw Anne differently, too. She wasn't unique any more --- simply one woman in a whole world of women. And I no longer felt ready to commit myself to spending an entire lifetime with her, as her partner.

My forebodings were all too fully justified. It was a very wretched week-end.   Anne was wholly unprepared for what I had to tell her, and took it very hard indeed. For her, nothing had changed; I was the lover of her choice, to whom she had confided her future, in spite of all obstacles.   She was not angry --- that wouldn't have been like her. She was simply terribly unhappy. It might have been easier if I'd been dumping her for another woman --- less of a blow to her self-esteem, maybe. But I wasn't --- I was simply moving on into a new life, and leaving her behind.

Anne went home.   The sense of relief I felt after she'd gone, told me I'd done the right thing...... for myself. For both of us? I don't know.   I've sometimes wondered what would have happened if Anne and I had gone on to try and build a life together.   It might have been a very good one. Anne would certainly have put all of herself into the attempt. I was the one who had still a long way to go, on the way to growing up.

I wrote to my parents that all was off with Anne, but that my other plans remained unchanged. My mother wrote back to say that she'd already heard from Anne. She told me to return to Anne the ring she'd given her, which Anne had left with me on her departure. I did this. I also got a nasty letter from Anne's mother, to which I didn't reply.   All of Mrs. Hoult's worst misgivings about me had come to pass. I don't blame her for feeling nasty about me.

And that was that. I saw Anne once again after that: about eight years later, in Israel. I heard of her a couple of times, over the years. But, for now, as I say ---- that was that.

~~~~~~~~~~~~~~~~~~~~~~

The days and weeks at The Grange went by. One week was much like the other, as far as our routine was concerned: work, argue, study, eat, sleep, work. It was a very healthy routine. Sickness was almost unknown among us. The hard work toughened our bodies wonderfully; I doubt if I've ever been so strong and physically fit in my life, before or since that time.   We developed intellectually, too.   The Grange had a library of hundreds of books of all kinds, most of them in English, reflecting the tastes and purposes of the trainees who had preceded us.   Almost everyone who came to The Grange added at least a book or two, or a gramophone record or two, to our library. Most of the books were what you could call "serious."

There was a lot of Jewish and Zionist history; a lot of political writing too --- most of it (predictably enough) left-leaning (it was here that I became acquainted with Victor Gollancz' "Left Book Club").

Much of the stuff I found unreadable; some of it was fascinating. I can remember some of the titles of books I read during that time: *The Floating Republic* (an account of mutiny in the British Navy during the Napoleonic Wars). *The Iron Heel* by Jack London (I was well acquainted with most of London's work). Several marvellous humorous books by Ludwig Bemelmans --- an American writer I'd never heard of before, but have loved and admired ever since. "*The Education of H*Y*M*A*N K*A*P*L*A*N*" by Leonard Q. Ross (Ross' real name, I learned later, is Leo Rosten). He is also the author of an immensely entertaining, scholarly book called "*The Joy of Yiddish*." I think the two "Kaplan" books are as good as anything by Mark Twain. We also had subscriptions to several newspapers and periodicals, which we read assiduously. I recall "The Daily Worker" and "The New Statesman and Nation."

When did I find time to read? I don't know. But I found time. We all did. Time was like money. You had to learn to make a very little go a long way.

All I have told you about The Grange so far has been of our life as a collective.   But we had individual lives too. I purposely don't use the word "private." At The Grange, the only things you could keep private --- so long as you didn't talk in your sleep! --- were your innermost thoughts.

The Grange had been functioning for several years, and all the country people around knew a great deal about us --- or supposed they did. There was this big house in which young unmarried men and women lived together, unsupervised.   "The Jews' 'ostel up at 't Grange? Oh, aye! Plenty of goings on up there, then, hey! Arrrh!" There was no malice in such remarks --- mostly wistful envy. Poor souls --- I think they would have found the truth very disappointing.

The truth is that we led lives of almost monastic austerity. If you think about it for a moment, you'll see that it couldn't have been otherwise. We were a public institution, sponsored by the Zionist Federation of Great Britain.   As prospective pioneers, we had a high profile in the Jewish community: children in the various Zionist youth movements were taught to admire and respect us, and to aspire one day to join us.   On the other hand, many people in the Jewish community harboured suspicions about us, just as lurid as those of the Berkshire locals (perhaps less benevolent), and would no doubt have rejoiced to see them confirmed. Any breath of scandal would have got us shut down, and done untold damage to the cause we served. We understood it was imperative that we appear impeccably respectable. And we took pains to do so.

Promiscuity was unknown among us. People who are sexually promiscuous usually need to talk about what they do; word would have got around in no time, and we couldn't have that. So there was no "screwing around."   Any sign of such a thing would have been dealt with quickly and finally. That does not mean that we all led celibate lives --- far from it. We were young, normal, healthy men and women. Hormones circulated vigorously in the bloodstreams of us all, and governed our behaviour to a much greater extent, I think, than we admitted to ourselves. But we kept our sexual activities shielded very carefully from the eyes of the outside world.

There was a lot of pairing off.   But these relationships, even when transient, were invariably monogamous; in fact, several of them led to marriage while I was at The Grange --- including that between Zara and myself, of which I shall tell shortly. There were unwritten rules to be observed. Any "private" doings had to take place in the individual's own time; there was no opting out of any of our collective activities.   All acknowledged couples were watched closely to make sure this was so; any sign of deviant behaviour met with severe disapproval. The most stridently vocal guardians of our collective integrity were quite often the unattached bachelors, understandably enough, I suppose. Sexual jealousy can have a potent effect on behavior, and the level of sexual tension in our community was very high, even though kept below the surface much of the time.

Overt acts associated with couples --- holding hands or kissing when anyone else was present, even sitting side by side at a group meeting --- were looked upon askance and generally avoided. In fact, if you didn't belong to the collective, you'd have found it hard to identify a going "couple." But there was plenty of undercover activity, nevertheless. Our drains were continually getting plugged up from having condoms flushed down them. The subject was regularly brought up at our general meetings, but it didn't do any good --- the blockages continued. Condoms were an important budget item.   In our records they were always referred to discreetly as "sundries"; we even came to call them that in ordinary conversation, and for years after The Grange, I used to think of a condom as a "sundry."   Even now, the term "sundried tomatoes" makes me smile.

When I arrived at The Grange there was one married couple in residence. They were a big public relations asset; nothing confers a stronger air of respectability than holy matrimony. Any parent or older person visiting us would always have their attention drawn to them. Actually, I don't remember what happened to them; by the time our group left for Israel, they had faded from the scene. But by then there were several more married couples, including Zara and myself. Now it is time for me to tell you about her.

4. Zara, love and marriage

I was twenty-two years old, and the hormones were racing through my veins, at a headlong pace which I recall now with almost incredulous wonder and delight. So it wasn't very long (it was no time at all, to be honest) before I found myself looking at the women in our commune, not only as comrades, but as women. None of them had been there long, and only one or two appeared to be attached to any particular male. I found them all terribly attractive. Hardly surprising --- they were interesting, unusual women. "Usual" women didn't make it to The Grange.

To some extent my ambivalence to Anne was that she was not there sharing this intense experience with me in the commune.   It was as if it was foreordained that I should pair off with one of the women in the group, because we were all now linked by an indissoluble bond. And whereas Anne was perhaps only a year or two younger than the others, I thought of my new acquaintances as women, fully developed and mature females.

The woman upon whom my interest soon became centred was Zara. She had already been there a few months --- long enough, she told me later, for a couple of the other bachelors to offer her their attentions. She had not encouraged them (I didn't know, then, just how discouraging Zara could be when she chose. Poor devils.........). With me, she was wary at first; after all, when I first arrived at The Grange, I'd been another girl's man. She had seen what had happened to Anne --- not something likely to make another woman rush to throw her arms around me. But the wariness wore off.

We found each other very congenial company, and began to seek each other out whenever possible. There wasn't an awful lot of opportunity. The only time we could get together *à deux* was after all the evening's programmes were over, and everybody else had staggered off to bed.   Then Zara and I would move to the kitchen and sit on the warm Aga stove, and talk. By then it would be very late; by the time we turned in, it would be much later still. The story of our courtship is a story of prolonged, extreme sleep deprivation.

I was fired up with love and lust for her, I could not function properly, it was impossible to hide my feelings, I wanted to be with Zara all the time. And what seemed so amazing was that she seemed to want the same thing, I suppose they call this love.   Zara was just eighteen years old when we met.   She was dark, even dark-skinned, with jet black short hair (in a way she reminded me of my mother).   She was vivacious, easy to laugh, and very, very sexy.   She had a wonderful figure, and I must admit having sleepless nights obsessing over how it might feel...

The tale of her parentage and early life is very different from mine.   Here it is in brief.   Zara's father, Sam Mischof, was born in Kemay (Kemaija), a small village near Kovno (Kaunas) in Lithuania (at that time, a part of the Russian Empire).   His family were smallholding peasants.   His mother kept a sort of inn, or boozing-ken (he told me this himself, many years later), which was patronized mostly by the non-Jewish peasants round about.   I remember Max's graphic description of helping his mother roll the insensible bodies of drunken peasants across the floor and out the door, before closing up on a Saturday night.   He must have then been about twelve years old.

In the early years of the 20th century, Max's father left Lithuania for America to seek a better life for himself and his family in *"Die Goldene Medineh"* --- "The Country of Gold."   They were to follow on, once he had established a foothold.   Like many others, Max's father was cheated by the person who sold him his passage on the boat. He ended up, not in America, but in Edinburgh, Scotland --- a destination for which the fare was much less than he'd paid. "I've a lot to thank that thieving bastard for" Sam said of the ticket-seller, seventy or eighty years later (Sam lived to be over a hundred years old). Scotland was always, for Sam Mischof, the finest country in the world, bar none; and the Scots, the finest people.

A year or two after the father's departure, Sam himself travelled to Edinburgh together with his elder sister. Quite an odyssey for a boy and girl barely into their teens, who knew no language but Yiddish, and had never before left their native village. I often think, how desperate must have been the fears and hopes which drove such people; how much courage and determination were needed, to make their enterprise succeed!......The children were helped, on arrival in Edinburgh, by members of the small Jewish community, who brought them into contact with their father. Sam was eventually apprenticed as a cabinet-maker. He worked hard, and prospered. By the start of WWII, in 1939, he owned and ran a furniture factory employing about 50 people.

About the year 1918, Sam got married to the daughter of Russian Jews who had come to Scotland in the previous century. Marie and her brothers, and her sister had been born in Scotland, and brought up mostly by their mother. Their father, an unworldly man, had been some kind of Talmudic scholar, unable to cope with the exigencies of keeping a family. He vanished from their ken quite early on. Zara said that as far as she knew, he had travelled to Palestine when it was still under Turkish rule, and died (probably of starvation, like many other poor people) in Jerusalem during WW1.

By heaven knows what prodigies of exertion and thrift, Zara's maternal grandmother succeeded in bringing up her children without the help of a husband and seeing that they got an education. One eventually received a Doctorate in Law from the University of Edinburgh, and had a distinguished career in the Scottish Civil Service. Another received his Doctorate in Science, and became a senior researcher for a great pharmaceutical company. The last one became a bus conductor, and a Communist. Marie did what Jewish girls were expected to do in those days: she got married. Zara was the youngest of 6 siblings and was born 1932. Life among the Mischofs during the 1920's and 1930's, while the children were growing up, seems to have been nothing short of hectic. Zara certainly recalled it as such.

From what Zara told me about herself, I gathered that childhood had not been easy or comfortable for her. Her mother, a prey to chronic ill-health, had found it increasingly difficult to manage her household. Neither Zara's sister Nanny, nor Zara herself, had been able to help her much, and their father was fully occupied with running his business. So that in the Mischkof home there prevailed a degree of anarchy probably greater than average. This was the picture, at any rate, that I got from Zara.

Whatever life was like in that home, one thing is clear. I have already mentioned a Jewish tradition of reverence for learning. This tradition was most scrupulously respected in the Mischkof family. The boys all attended Heriot's, one of the highest-regarded boy's schools in Edinburgh. They were not sent there to enhance their social status, but in order to ensure that they got the best education available. After graduating from high school, all of them went on to university to learn a profession.

Zara was also sent to a famous school: Gillespie's (known to many as the setting for "*The Prime of*

Miss Jean Brodie"). It was while Zara was a pupil at this school, aged seventeen, that her mother died, after years of being a near-helpless invalid. This was a turning-point in Zara's life. Not long after her mother's death, Zara left home and made her way to The Grange.

From the way she spoke to me about them, it was clear that Zara had great difficulty in coming to terms with her feelings about her family, especially her father. She was intensely attached to him; at the same time, she deeply resented what she considered shortcomings in his behavior towards his family, and towards her mother in particular. She blamed him for not having done enough, in her view, to make her mother's life easier during her illness.

This emotional ambivalence affected Zara's relations with everyone close to her. If she loved someone, she gave them her loyalty without reservation, and expected the same in return. The more deeply attached she was to a person, the more intensely she felt aggrieved at any behavior which she found wanting in loyalty. Disloyalty towards those you professed to love was, for her, the worst sin in the world.

I was fascinated with Zara. It wasn't just physical attraction, although there was plenty of that. Zara was a woman of very high intelligence, with a razor-sharp critical faculty. She enjoyed watching people's behavior, and analyzing it, and getting at the motives underlying it. Her skill at doing this was astonishing, and at times disconcerting, even at that age (she was only eighteen at the time, remember). People rarely fooled her for long: she had no time for sham and posturing, and could see through those very easily as a rule. I enjoyed having her share her insights with me. In later years they became clearer and more profound, as her powers of observation grew with practice and experience. I think Zara could have been a brilliant psychoanalyst. I learned more from her about what makes people tick than from anyone else I've ever known.

Zara found me attractive too (if she hadn't, I'd have known about it very quickly). We became more and more wrapped up in each other. We tried not to be obtrusive about it, but apparently not with much success. We soon found ourselves the object of considerable criticism from our group --- voiced, as usual, frequently and loudly. There were complicating factors. Sexual jealousy was one. Much of the criticism directed at us was born of jealousy, and was full of malice --- nasty stuff indeed, intended simply to hurt, not to help us do better by the group. Also, I think some of Anne's friends suspected Zara of having taken advantage of Anne's absence, to insinuate herself into my affections and cut Anne out. This was not true. It was I who sought out Zara, not the reverse. She was actually very shy, and I found the early stages of our courtship quite hard going.

Anyway, as time passed, Zara and I found ourselves a highly unpopular couple. At one point we seriously considered asking the powers-that-be of the Movement, to let us transfer to another training collective (there were two other such groups, on farms in Sussex). We even talked about leaving the Movement altogether. It was a very stressful time for both of us. It brought us even closer together.

Things got better when Zara and I asked and were eventually given permission (after having endured a lot more public criticism, at the general meeting at which our request was inevitably discussed) to move into a room of our own. For one thing, it was a private place, where we could be together out of sight of the group. For another, we started getting a lot more sleep, which made both of us stronger and less vulnerable. And in addition, help came for us from outside, in a most unexpected way.

In no time at all, the powers-that-be at *Habonim* headquarters in London became aware that at The Grange, a couple had moved into married quarters without benefit of clergy. Post-haste, a Big Wheel arrived, in the shape of Arnold.   Arnold addressed us at a general meeting, and gave us an official dressing-down. He pointed out the awful danger of what we were doing, the possibility of a scandal with much attendant negative publicity. He laid down the law. Zara and I were to move back into bachelor quarters, and stay there until such time as our union was officially sanctified.

To Zara's and my surprise and gratification, the entire group rose as one in our defence. We were responsible adult members of the commune, exercising our free will with the consent of our group, and no one from outside the collective was going to dictate to us what we could or couldn't do --- least of all, the powers-that-be in the London office of *Habonim*.   One after another of our comrades arose and spoke in the same vein --- among them, some of our fiercest critics.   Arnold went back to London with a very large flea in his ear.

Short of disowning or disbanding the entire collective, there wasn't much that he or the powers-that-be could do --- and they certainly weren't going to do *that;* such a step would create, if anything, an even bigger scandal than the one they were trying to avoid. And Zara and I found that our status in the collective had changed. We were no longer recalcitrant individuals defying a hostile community; we were members of the *kibbutz* under threat from outside, and the entire group had moved to close ranks around us. Our lives became much easier from that time on. Things got even better, as other couples were established, and pairing off became more socially acceptable. Attention was no longer focused upon us.

One thing this incident did was to cause Zara and me to give serious thought to our future together. Everything Arnold had scolded us about was, in fact, true. We were indeed jeopardizing the good name of *Habonim* by living at The Grange *en famille*; and if we had any sort of serious intentions toward each other, the sooner we made good on them, the better it would be for everyone. So we considered getting married: and both of us found the idea to our liking. We had been living together for several months by this time.

Zara got leave to go to Edinburgh, to attend her sister's wedding. She took advantage of this event to tell her father that she had met a man whom she wanted to marry. His first words in response were: "Is he a Yid?" to which one of her brothers, who was present, replied before she could open her mouth "Of course he is. Look where she met him! What else would he be except a Yid?" [the name "Yid" is used contemptuously by non-Jews when referring to, or addressing, a Jew. When used by an Ashkenazi (European) Jew like Zara's father, it is simply a Yiddish word meaning "Jew"]. This appeared to convince Zara's father. It was important that he be so convinced, for if he knew I wasn't a Jew, he would withhold his consent to our marrying. We needed that consent --- in writing --- because at that time, the age of legal majority in Britain was 21; Zara was still, in law, a minor. So Zara came back to The Grange with instructions to bring me to Edinburgh, for a parental once-over.

We took an overnight train that got us into Waverley Station at about 5:30 am. When we arrived at her home nobody was up yet. We sat down in the kitchen. I took a desultory mouthful or two of the cornflakes which Zara gave me. I was quite nervous, and didn't feel much like eating. After a while a small, balding man in undershirt, trousers (suspenders dangling down) and slippers came in. Zara said "Hello, Daddy," kissed him, and introduced me. He shook my hand perfunctorily, seeming hardly to look at me, mumbled something inarticulate, and went over to shave in the kitchen sink, his back to me.

My feelings of general discomfort were multiplied tenfold, when I suddenly realized that I was being minutely scrutinized by a single, unblinking eye, reflected in Mr. Mischkof's shaving mirror. That expressionless, penetrating gaze unnerved me completely. I sat dumb and motionless, while the cornflakes grew soggy in my bowl. Mr. Mischkof finished shaving and went back to his room. A little later he emerged, neatly dressed in business suit, clean shirt and tie, and carefully polished shoes, and went out of the house. By this time I was totally discombobulated and near-paralytic. I can't remember if he said anything, or indeed if he took any notice of me at all. After a while I was able to begin breathing normally again, but I never managed to finish those cornflakes.

Some weeks later, Zara and I were married in Reading. We were married twice, three days apart. For Zara's father's sake, we had to be married in a synagogue. Anything else would be no marriage in his eyes. But to be married in a synagogue, one had to be a Jew: which I wasn't. My cover story, that I was at The Grange training to be a Jewish pioneer in Israel, seemed to be enough to convince the *hazan* (cantor) of the Reading synagogue of my *bona fides* as a Jew --- though from the way he looked at me, Zara and I were pretty certain that he had his doubts. But if so, he kept them to himself. He married us by Jewish ritual at the Reading synagogue, under the traditional *huppah* or wedding canopy, with Zara's father and a handful of our comrades in attendance.

The *hazan* was empowered by the Government to act as registrar on its behalf, and to register our marriage in the Civil Register. However, since we were getting married under false pretences, Zara and I were afraid that this might invalidate the ceremony, not only in Jewish law (which was certainly the case), but in English civil law as well. Wanting to take no chances, we had therefore already married, by civil ceremony, three days previously (on June 14, 1951) at the Reading registry office, with two of our comrades acting as witnesses. Our occupations were entered in the register as "cook" and "farm labourer" respectively.

So Zara and I ended up as married as married could be, with two certificates to prove it, one in English, the other in Hebrew and Aramaic. I have them both in safe keeping still.

Whatever suspicions Mr. Mischkof may have had about my identity and forbears, he chose (like the Reading *hazan*) to keep them to himself, and give me the benefit of the doubt. Several years were to pass before he learned for certain that his daughter was married to a *goy*. He told me the story a long time afterward. The news was broken to him by one of his "friends" in Edinburgh; she told him (with great relish, he said) that the fact was common knowledge in the Edinburgh Jewish community, and that he might as well know it too. This act of thoughtfulness did nothing to endear that lady to my father-in-law. "She was a crooked businesswoman" he told me, "and should have gone to jail. But she let her husband go instead. Aye, poor bastard."

By the time I heard the story, Zara's family had long since become my family too, and Mr. Mischkof was "Dad"; and my being a *goy* mattered not at all. "As far as I'm concerned, you're as much a Jew as any of my children," he would say to me in later years, "and more of one than some of them."

Before moving to Israel, I asked at *Habonim* Head Office what I should write in my *aliyah* application; they told me that if I wrote anything else but "Jewish," things might be more complicated for me; so I swallowed any misgivings, and wrote "Jewish" wherever I had to.   And sure enough, things remained very simple. When I got to Israel and eventually exchanged my *te'udat oleh* for an ID card, the card said "Jewish." It still does. Who am I to argue!

~~~~~~~~~~~~~~~~~~~~~~~~~~~

The seasons went by.   In the winter, there isn't a lot you can do in the fields on a farm in England, other than hedging and ditching; consequently, most of us would find ourselves doing a variety of non-farming jobs at one time or other. I worked for some months as a builder's labourer, building an experimental piggery for the Ministry of Agriculture. I spent some time pruning the King's spruce trees in the Royal forests at Windsor. The 14-mile bike ride to work, over icy roads, sometimes through a snowstorm, and mostly in the dark, was a nightmare which took several hours each way (the winter of 1951-1952 was exceptionally harsh).

I became expert at falling off the bike without breaking anything but my thermos bottle. On the job itself, one stood with a long-handled saw under a tree, cutting off the lower branches close to the trunk. One had to be looking up all the time, while the snow in the branches kept getting dislodged and falling down inside one's collar. Thank goodness, I only lasted a month at that one: I could never make it to work on time.

I worked as a bench fitter in a small factory which made agricultural machinery --- machines for planting potatoes, others for harvesting them. I acquired skills which I'd never dreamed existed. When the weather grew milder and there was work to be had in agriculture, I planted thousands and thousands of iris tubers, in the fields of a famous flower-growing concern called Waterer's. I spread human manure on the fields of Mr. Harry Westacott. Westacott bought the stuff by the truckload from a nearby sewage treatment plant. He farmed about a thousand acres, and used a lot of manure.

The trucks would drive slowly to and fro across the fields, while a crew of three (including myself) walked behind, dragging the "activated sludge" off the tail of the truck, using long-handled rakes. The contents of the sludge were an astonishingly detailed artefactual record of the social life of the population of Berkshire. No doubt an anthropologist would have found the study of them very rewarding. I didn't. Naturally, the stuff fell right in our path, and by the end of the day we'd be covered in it. The smell of it got up your nostrils and stayed there. Even after I'd got home, and showered interminably with hot water and lots of soap, and put on clean clothes, everything still smelled of activated sludge. That was the most disagreeable job I ever had to do during those years. I *always* washed my hands before eating my sandwiches, on that job.

One thing that grew stronger with the passage of time was my respect for my English fellow-workers. I watched them toil for long hours, doing work which was hard, usually dull, and sometimes back-breaking. The material rewards they reaped were meagre; the conditions under which they and their families lived were modest at best, wretchedly squalid at worst. Unlike myself and my fellow would-be pioneers at The Grange, they had no brave ideal to sustain them, no lofty purpose to strengthen their backs and lift up their spirits under the burden of unending labour; moreover, there was very little hope of their situation ever being much different. This was the stuff their lives were made of; this was what they would continue doing, all their days. I watched them get on with it, usually cheerful and uncomplaining; striving, most of them, to give an honest day's work in return for their pay. And I saw how, when the day's work was over, they would find all sorts of ways of making life more pleasant and enjoyable, despite the slender resources they had.

Most of my English fellow-workers were very conscious of their good fortune, to be living in post-war Britain with a Socialist government --- under which a working man could feel that he had some measure of influence, however slight, over the running of his country.   What must it have been like, I wonder, to be a working man in an earlier age, in a society built on hereditary privilege, ruled by people who used you, while despising you and all your class, and making no secret of the fact ---- *("give them a bath-tub and they'll keep coal in it")* --- people who maintained their rule by means of a very English blend of pious brain-washing *("God bless the Squire and his relations, and keep us in our proper stations")*, and the constant threat (for the trouble-maker) of the jail-house, the cat, and the gallows; and for good measure, an occasional whiff of grapeshot. It must have been awful. Why didn't

Britain have a bloody social revolution like France or Russia? Not, I think, because the British ruling classes were less deserving of one than were the French, or the Russian; they were simply luckier. English working people are more good-natured, and more easily put upon, than those of most other nations.

Zara's experience of work was as varied as mine. One job she had was at a famous jam factory, whose name was a household word in Britain. The work she had to do was numbingly brainless. One task entailed sitting in front of a moving belt, on which countless oranges passed endlessly in front of you: you had to pick out those with a calyx still attached (that is the little green button where the stalk joins the orange), and remove this with a metal plectrum attached to the end of one finger. Another task was to watch yet another moving belt, along which empty jars passed under a spout, which filled each one automatically. You had to make sure that there was a jam-jar in every one of the positions on the belt; for the jam came out of the spout, regardless. This particular job was reserved for the intellectual heavyweights, for if anything went wrong (said Zara), as it occasionally did, the resulting mess was indescribable.

Work in the jam factory was so incredibly dull, besides being poorly paid, that most of the people doing it were, Zara told me, quite literally mentally retarded; anyone of normal intelligence very quickly went round the bend, in the manner of Charlie Chaplin in "*Modern Times.*" After a couple of weeks, Zara couldn't stand it any longer, and got permission from the *kibbutz* work committee to resign and find another job. She couldn't eat jam for many years thereafter.

One job Zara enjoyed --- probably because it was a real test of intelligence and skill --- was at a factory which made communications equipment for aircraft. They had big orders from the R.A.F. It was the time of the Berlin Airlift. This was before the age of printed circuits: the baseboard for each radio was assembled by hand, and all the connections were made of fine wire which was soldered into place. Zara turned out to have an uncanny skill at reading the most complex circuit diagrams, and getting all the connections right first time. The work was piece-work, and for a while, Zara was bringing in more money every week than any other member of the commune. But that wasn't what we were there for: we were preparing ourselves for a life on the land, and as soon as the weather improved, back to the land Zara went.

Her new job was at Elisha J. Hicks' Rose Gardens. Mr. Hicks was a renowned breeder of roses, who boasted many of the county's most distinguished families among his clientele. He was very kind to Zara. So was his son Fred --- but it soon became obvious that Fred's kindness was a calculated ploy, and that he was actually After Only One Thing. He pursued this objective with all the avid single-mindedness of a true latter-day satyr. Zara (and her friend Una, who also worked for Hicks, and was also the object of Fred's lubricious attentions) spent a lot of time and effort keeping Fred at arm's length, while trying to avoid provoking a crisis.

I think they both must have done this with consummate skill. The accounts Zara used to give me in the evening, of the day's chase, and her evasive manoeuvres, were hilarious. This situation came to an end for Zara, when the *kibbutz* decided to appoint her *"Economit,"* or cook-housekeeper, for the commune. She told Mr. Hicks that she was leaving to get married. He was sorry to see her go, and gave her a substantial cash bonus (I think it was several days' pay) as a wedding present. Fred's reaction is not on record.

~~~~~~~~~~~~~~~~~~~~~~

Nothing in my life, before or since, has ever been quite like those two years at The Grange.   And I think that most of those who shared that experience feel pretty much the same.   One felt so very much *alive.*   Perhaps in part, this was because everything we did, however insignificant, however seemingly trivial, was all bent to the same purpose: preparing ourselves for a new life, in a new Land. Nothing that we did was without meaning; not a single moment of our lives was frittered away.   In addition, the closeness into which we were forced by our way of life, had its effect upon us all.

We became more mutually tolerant, as we grew to know and understand each other better.   The endless discussions, in which we analyzed each other at excruciating length, grew shorter and fewer. We all knew each other too well for there to be any point in going over the same ground, again and yet again.   We began to achieve a degree of harmony.   Each of us knew pretty well what was expected of him --- or of her --- by the others, and did it without fuss. We were developing the ability to function effectively as a group.

As for Zara and me --- the difficult period in our relations with the group was behind us. We were happy, with the collective and with each other. It was a good time.   Several other couples got married. Once, Zara and I even managed an afternoon off. The communal budget included a personal allowance for each of us; not exactly a princely sum --- I think it was a penny a week (about two cents US). If allowed to accumulate over a year for two people, this amounts to almost ten shillings. I don't recall how we managed to get the time off work --- it may have been on a Saturday afternoon. We took the bus into Reading, a sizable town about seven miles away, and went to a cinema matinée. The movie showing was "*The African Queen.*" Afterwards, we went and had tea and cakes at a tea-shop nearby, and then went home. It was a wonderful outing.

Zara and I never got the second year's afternoon off which was coming to us; for it suddenly became necessary for us to depart The Grange, and the shores of Britain, in great haste. I was liable for National Service --- two years' conscription in His Majesty's forces. While I was a student, my conscription had been deferred; but now the Ministry of Labour and National Service finally caught up with me. I was summoned to a medical examination, found fit for service, and instructed to go home and wait for my call-up notice, which, I was told, might take a couple of weeks to arrive.

We had to act very fast. If the call-up papers arrived while I was still at The Grange (or anywhere on British soil) I'd have no choice but to answer them; not to do so would make me a deserter. If I were already out of the country when the papers arrived, I'd be off the hook; only British subjects actually resident in Britain were liable for National Service. All of us in the collective were agreed that no purpose of ours would be served by my spending the next two years "square-bashing." We had a different agenda.

I made some inquiries and cabled my parents. For some time, they'd been trying to persuade Zara and me to travel to Chile for a visit; they'd never met her, and were anxious to do so before we vanished over the horizon into the mysterious East. The cheapest way to travel, I found out, was by boat. There were berths available on a passenger vessel leaving England in three or four days: the third-class fare to Buenos Aires was £70 per person. My father wired his bank in London; and about eight days after my medical exam, Zara and I were at Southampton, boarding R.M.S. *Alcántara* en route for Buenos Aires. We were to be met on arrival by a business associate of my father's; he would help us get to Chile. Our plans were not too definite; we reckoned that after a visit of three or four months, we would leave Chile and rejoin our comrades, who by that time should already be in Israel. We made this clear to my parents, who I thought might be making other plans for us.

It was Zara's first sea voyage (I had been back and forward across the Atlantic several times). It was a wonderful journey --- a belated honeymoon --- full of interesting people and events. There was Viktor, the Polish refugee, who had schemed for three years to escape the socialist paradise, finally stealing a fishing boat at Gdansk, and getting picked up by a Swedish freighter in the Baltic. Viktor spoke nothing but Polish, but managed to communicate remarkably fluently with gestures and inarticulate sounds, and a few words of what he fondly imagined was German. He told us bits of his life story; how he'd been a jeweller in Warsaw, like his father before him, until the Communists came and he lost everything.

He was going to Brazil, where he had relatives in São Paulo who would help him get back on his feet. He had a refugee's *laissez-passer* from the Vatican in lieu of a passport, and whenever the ship docked, the police wouldn't let him go ashore, until Zara and I promised to be responsible for him. He attached himself to us like a little dog. When we parted at Rio, he tearfully begged us to come and visit him in Brazil once he'd made his fortune. "I will give you a brief-case full of jewels. You will take it to Europe and sell the jewels, and simply return the cost to me. The profits will be for you. There is no risk; nobody will think to examine you, you look so innocent." I think that's what he said. I think he might very well have meant it, too --- at least at the time. Later, in Chile, we got a letter from him; but I didn't know anyone there who could read Polish, and by the time we reached Israel the letter was lost, forever unread.

For the first few days of the journey there were only a handful of third-class passengers. But at Vigo, and later at Lisbon, several hundred Spanish and Portuguese emigrants came aboard ---- poor peasants, mostly, travelling to South America at their Governments' expense, in the hope of finding a better life than their own countries had to offer. They were very simple people: many of them had never seen the sea (or a shower, or a flushing toilet, either --- they certainly had no idea how to use these facilities; nor could they read the signs which said "Señoras" and "Caballeros," respectively.).

Once we were out into the Atlantic they all became seasick for the rest of the voyage. They were crowded in dormitories, fifty or sixty together (how glad Zara and I were, that we'd had the presence of mind to get a cabin to ourselves, even if it *had* cost my father an additional ten pounds or so!). When the dormitories became unbearable (they must have been hell, especially in the tropics --- we had to pass the open door of one, to get to our cabin), they came on deck, and sat or squatted hour after hour leaning disconsolately against the bulkheads, occasionally puking listlessly on to the deck in front of them. The crew had to roust them out and wash the deck down several times a day.

I wonder how many of these unfortunates found the better life they were looking for. Not very many, I suspect. A few months later, when Zara and I returned to Europe, the third-class dormitories of our ship were packed with hundreds of these same European peasants, being repatriated, after not finding what they had dreamed of.

We were met on the dockside at Buenos Aires by an old associate of my father's from his insurance company, an Argentinian. "I am glad of an opportunity to help you," he told me. "I owe a great deal to your father. When he resigned his position with the Company eighteen years ago, the people at Head Office in England asked him to recommend a successor. The English managers here naturally thought that one of them would get the promotion --- never an Argentinian.   They looked upon your father as a sort of traitor when he nominated me. But he did so, nevertheless."

We had to stay in Buenos Aires for several days: the weather over the Andes was very bad, and all transandine flights were suspended.   We were wined and dined by my father's friend, and by my cousin Diane, who was at that time living in Buenos Aires, and had also come to greet us at the dock, on learning from my mother that we were coming.

And of course --- there was Yoash's uncle.

~~~~~~~~~~~~~~~~~~~~~~~~

The day before Zara and I left The Grange, Yoash, one of our fellow-members of the commune, said to me: "If you're going to be in Buenos Aires, will you look up my uncle and say 'hello' for me?" Yoash had been among the *kindertransporten*: some thousands of Jewish children from Germany and Austria, who had been admitted, not long before the war began, into England as refugees, to be looked after by foster families. One day when he was about nine or ten, Yoash had been taken by his parents in Germany to a railway station and put on a train which took him to England. He never saw his family again. By the end of the war they were all dead.

Except apparently for this uncle, who had somehow got away and now lived in Buenos Aires. After the war, one of the organizations which helped Holocaust survivors had put the two in touch with each other. They had never met.

On our second day in Buenos Aires, Zara and I were strolling down a broad avenue when I saw a street sign: *Avenida de Mayo.* I stopped and said to Zara: "I remember the address Yoash gave me --- it was *Avenida de Mayo 811.* Now we're here, let's see if we can find Yoash's uncle."

No. 811 was an office building. Among the nameplates was: *Arturo Mayer. 2º piso.* We went upstairs and knocked on a frosted glass door. An impersonal voice said *"Adelante!"* There was a middle-aged, bespectacled man behind a desk. His look was as cold and blank as the frosted glass. I addressed him in Spanish, and said we brought greetings from Yoash. He looked up uncomprehending. *Who?* "We're friends of your nephew Yoash," I said. "Harry Kahn. From England."

The response was instant, and amazing in its intensity. He was up and out of his chair and around the desk in one bound. "*Harry?* You are friends of Harry? You know him? From England?" He threw his arms around each of us in turn. He was beside himself with excitement and emotion. How long had we known Harry? What was Harry doing? Where was he? What did he look like? The questions came tumbling out one after the other. What were we doing in Buenos Aires? What could he do for us? What were our plans? He would take us out to lunch. He shut up the office there and then. From that moment on he couldn't see enough of us. He was unmarried, and so far as we could see, didn't have much in the way of friends. It saddens me even now, to think of the desolation of loneliness in which this man must have lived --- on his own in an alien land, speaking an alien tongue, his memories all of a world cruelly destroyed, nothing left to him but ghosts.

And of course, Yoash. It was clear that the thought of Yoash sustained Mr. Mayer, gave him a reason for living, a link to the life he had once known, a life with family, friends, a future, hope...... and we were his ambassadors from Yoash. He couldn't do enough for us. Between the hospitality of Mr. Mayer, Diane, and my father's friend, we were reduced, by our fourth day in Buenos Aires, to remaining in our hotel room and eating nothing but bicarbonate of soda.   Heaven knows what would have become of us if the weather had not improved, and flights to Chile resumed.   We continued on our way.

Before proceeding with our story, I want to tell you the end of the story of Yoash and his uncle. It's happier than the beginning. The following year, back in England, I told Yoash about meeting Mr. Mayer, and tried to get across to him how important a part he had in his uncle's life. That probably wasn't necessary; I think it was a two-way thing --- Yoash didn't have anyone much of his own, either, other than his uncle. Anyway, many years later, Yoash told me that he'd kept in communication with Mr. Mayer, and had eventually gone to visit him in Buenos Aires.

They were able, apparently, to establish an affectionate relationship, and visited each other a number of times. When Yoash's uncle died, he left all his worldly goods to his nephew (who had remained, eventually, in England); and Yoash found himself quite a rich man. This was just as well, for he was by then afflicted with a variety of ailments (Parkinson's disease and diabetes among them), and couldn't work or look after himself. With his uncle's inheritance, he could afford to get proper care. I was saddened to learn not long ago (December 2000) that Yoash had finally succumbed to his manifold illnesses. I learned, also, that I wasn't quite right in saying he had no-one in the world but his uncle --- it turned out that he had some sort of cousins in Israel. I should have remembered that just about every Jew in the world has some sort of cousins in Israel. That's one of the reasons Israel exists.

~~~~~~~~~~~~~~~~~~~~~~~

It was only five years since I'd left home to travel to England; and yet it felt as though I'd been away for half a lifetime or more. I suppose that was because so much had happened to me in the meantime. Zara and I stayed with my parents, at the same house in Villa Alemana where I'd spent many of my boyhood years. My parents were delighted at meeting Zara; I don't know what they'd expected, but anyway they loved her. My old friends were all glad to see me, and to welcome Zara and me back into their circle.

I found myself temporary jobs to do, so that Zara and I could have a little spending money. Zara spent her time getting to know my parents (that was the chief reason we'd come to Chile, after all), my friends, and the country I'd grown up in. While we were there, my brother Larry got married to Marcia, an American; her father was an engineer, who managed a large textile factory for the Chilean owners.

She was a beautiful red-headed girl. Zara and I didn't have the kind of clothes suitable for attending a wedding, so my mother had an outfit tailored for each of us. Zara had a light blue dress with a little hat and veil; she looked lovely. I had a grey double-breasted suit. It is the only made-to-measure article of clothing I've ever possessed. Zara and I enjoyed ourselves greatly in Chile. The fact was not lost on my parents, who made various gentle overtures to try and persuade us to stay for good.

But we knew that we were simply marking time; Chile held no future for us. After a few months, Zara and I let my parents know that we were ready to move on. They were saddened, but did not make a fuss. My father got us passage on an Italian passenger boat ("Antoniotto Usodimare") from Valparaiso to Barcelona, and gave us a few dollars; more, probably, than he could spare. With those, and with what little we had of our own, we reckoned we could make it back across Spain and France, to England. There, we would pack our "Aliyah Boxes," say our goodbyes, and finally set out for Israel.

~~~~~~~~~~~~~~~~~~~~~~~

I love sea travel. There are so many wonderful experiences awaiting one who travels by sea. In fine weather you can stand for hour after hour, right up in the bow of the ship, and look down at the porpoises who race along with you, occasionally edging up to the ship's cutwater and scratching themselves against it. Time ceases to mean anything. Then there are the sounds. On board ship there is no silence, and no stillness. You are surrounded by unceasing sound and movement --- they are always there, even though for long periods you may not notice them. Laying in your bunk at night you perceive them intensely --- you can feel the whole ship alive, murmuring, pulsating all around you.

When you go ashore after a few days at sea, the world --- however noisy --- seems strangely motionless and void. I feel sorry for those people whose bodies revolt against sea travel, or who are denied it by circumstance. They miss experiences which can be very profoundly satisfying. I feel lucky to have had them. Travel on a commercial air liner is by comparison unutterably dreary and boring. Its only redeeming feature (I suppose that must be considered a redeeming feature) is that it gets you quickly where you need to go. As far as I'm concerned, the most spiritually uplifting experience that air travel provides, is the feel of a tot of Drambuie going down my throat, and reconciling me to my meal. Sometimes it takes two tots. Sometimes there's no Drambuie.

Zara and I both remembered that journey back to England as one of the most fascinating experiences of our lives. It was even more fraught with exciting incident, and interesting people, than the outward journey. And we were in the best possible situation to make the most of the experience: young, healthy, carefree, happy with each other, ready and eager for the adventure of our lives in Israel. Looking back, I think also that our youth and innocence were like a sort of charm, shielding us from harm.

Our travelling companions were a variegated lot. Most of the third class passengers were Spanish and Italian emigrants who had failed to make it in the New World and were being repatriated. But there were also others, more interesting. At meals Zara and I shared a table with a couple in late middle age, whose names I don't remember. They had come to Chile as young peasant emigrants from some village in Italy, many years before. Things had gone well for them: their *almacén* (grocery store) had prospered. Now, comfortably retired, they were going back to visit their former home, and to show off their success to their admiring families and the friends of their youth. They were good-natured, kindly people. Both of them were very fat and ate prodigiously.

The food on board was simple, Italian, and delicious. It was on that journey that I learned to know, and to love, aubergines (*melanzane*) and garlic (*aglio*) --- two marvellous foodstuffs which we never ate at home, because our mother didn't like them. There was always a carafe (constantly replenished) of rough, red *vino di pasto* on the table. Sometimes in my youthful *hubris* I would drink glass for glass with the fat gentleman; at the end of the meal, since he was two or three times my size, the concentration of alcohol in my veins would, naturally, be double or treble what it was in his, and I would stagger away to sleep it off. Zara was very forbearing. The only time she got angry was when I spent the whole of our brief call at

Curaçao in a vinous postprandial stupor, and she had to go ashore alone.

An interesting travelling companion was August, the ethnic Indian who came aboard at Curaçao (he had a Hindu name, but asked us to call him August, for simplicity's sake). He had a shop in Curaçao: the "Oriental Palace Bazaar." His stories of a shopkeeper's life were immensely entertaining. His account of helping an American tourist lady try on a brassière without taking her clothes off, was memorably hilarious. August was with Zara and me when we missed the ship at Tenerife; we succeeded in catching up with it by the skin of our teeth, with the good-natured assistance of the crew of the harbour-master's launch. It turned out, luckily for us, that a V.I.P. passenger had missed the ship too, and the captain hove to outside the harbour when he saw the launch, thinking we were the V.I.P.

This episode depleted our already meagre exchequer, to the extent that Zara and I arrived in Barcelona with not enough money for our train fare to London. We bought tickets to Paris, checked in our luggage, and spent the night before our journey in the streets of Barcelona, ending up on the coldest park bench I have ever tried unsuccessfully to sleep on (it was a great stone slab, like the ones in the morgue in TV thrillers). On arrival in Paris, I spent the last of our funds on a phone call to our fellow-pioneer Frank, who we knew was working for *Habonim* in London.

Luckily, Frank was in the office when I phoned, and gave me the address of his opposite number in the Paris branch of *Habonim*, who Frank said owed him some money. From this individual we were able to get money for our fares to London, and for our first square meal since arriving in Barcelona several days earlier (we weren't actually starving. We'd eaten a baguette and a tin of anchovies on the train to Paris, but still we were pretty ravenous). I can remember every detail of that dinner in Paris, it was so good: we had lamb chops and braised potatoes, and a glass of *vin rouge* apiece. It cost us 300 old francs each. We were also able to kip down for the night at youth movement headquarters; finally, at long last, we got on the train, and after an uneventful journey (for a change) arrived at Waterloo station, within a taxi-ride of friends and shelter.

We stayed only a few days in England. There was a flying visit to Edinburgh, to say goodbye to Zara's father. While we were there, Zara's brother-in-law, a trade union official, gave us a couple of tickets to watch the Coronation procession from a grandstand opposite Buckingham Palace gate (he couldn't go, he said, because he was in mourning for his father who had died shortly before). It was an excellent vantage point. The stream of kings, presidents, dignitaries, went on interminably. I remember Queen Salote of Tonga: she was the biggest woman I've ever seen, with a smile to match. She seemed to be overflowing her open carriage as she passed us laughing and waving.

After the princes and the prime ministers came crowds of Field-Marshals, Admirals, Major-Generals, Air Marshals, as thick as flies on fresh manure. Most of the Imperial General Staff must have been there. Many of them were on foot. And speaking of fresh manure, there was an awful lot of it on the road by this time, since there were no motor cars: all the vehicles were horse-drawn. The sight of these unfortunate gentlemen, in their uniforms heavy with gold braid, hopping and skipping desperately over the steaming heaps of horse-shit, was as good as a scene from Gilbert and Sullivan. They weren't always quite nimble enough. Westminster Abbey must have smelt like a stable that day. When the procession had passed, Zara and I returned to the *Habonim* clubhouse to watch the Coronation on TV, and handed our grandstand tickets on to Frank, who went with a friend to see the procession returning to the Palace.

On the following day we departed.   Goodbye, England; hello, Israel.

5. In the Land, life on the *kibbutz*

Our arrival in Israel was undramatic. Nobody sang, nobody wept, nobody fell down to kiss the blessed soil of the Land. We just gathered our stuff and got off the boat. One thing happened of which I didn't take much notice at the time; later, in retrospect, it became more significant. On our way through the dingy sheds of Haifa port, I found myself standing before a nondescript person, who unceremoniously stuck some sort of tube up the leg of my shorts, and before I knew what was happening, blasted my private parts with a cloud of grayish-white dust. I later learned that this treatment was accorded to all immigrants whose passage was paid for out of public funds. If you'd bought your own ticket, you were allowed to enter the Holy Land with your privacy inviolate and your *mandavoshkes* (a Yiddish word meaning "pubic lice") unmolested.

Years later, Charley Beeton, a young man of Moroccan origin who got elected to the Knesset on an ethnic protest ticket (the "Black Panthers"), used this experience to epitomize the contemptuous, discriminatory treatment that he and fellow-Moroccans received at the hands of the Israel establishment.   "We were greeted with DDT!" he would shout. He was right enough about the contemptuous treatment; but Moroccan immigrants weren't the only ones who had their testicles dusted on arrival.

There is a moral to this story: if you are a louse, and come to settle in Israel, be careful to batten only on people who paid their own way here----you may live longer.

Zara and I were met at the port by Moshe with a van.   During the time we were at The Grange, Moshe had been at one of the other two training farms operated in England by our youth movement.   Groups from all three farms had combined and come to Israel together, with the object of either founding a new *kibbutz*, or joining an already existing *kibbutz* as reinforcement. There were about 70 in all, in our *garin* or settlement group. We were to undergo a "settling-in" period of a few months at *Kibbutz* Gal-Ed in the Galilee, during which we could begin to learn Hebrew, adjust to living and working conditions in Israel, and have a look around, to see what permanent settlement options were available to us.

Our comrades, who had already been in Gal-Ed several months, greeted Zara and me warmly, and showed us to our quarters: one room in a *tzrif*, or wooden hut. It was one of a cluster of half-a-dozen similar structures, all occupied by members of our group. Every *tzrif* had two or three rooms, each one occupied by either a married couple or two bachelors.

There weren't enough huts for everyone in the group: some of our comrades lived in tents. The rooms had electric light; if you'd come to Israel with a table lamp, or a radio, there'd be a socket to plug them in to (if you hadn't, too bad - nobody was handing those things out). Hygienic facilities --- showers, toilets, etc., were communal; you walked to them. Outside every cluster of huts there'd usually be a water-tap. The whole situation had a nice "pioneer-ish" feel to it which was very acceptable to us, and not in the least daunting. Our two years' training in England had prepared us for almost anything.

Not, however, for the bed-bugs. Neither Zara nor I had ever encountered a bed-bug. That night we were almost eaten alive. Next day our comrades explained, laughing, that everyone had been through this; these wooden huts were peculiarly prone to infestation by bugs.   They showed us what remedial action was available: this consisted in more or less marinating the entire hut in kerosene, from roof to floor. We did what had to be done, and the bugs backed off to some extent. I doubt if anything short of burning the place to the ground would have got rid of them entirely.

Kibbutz Gal-Ed is located about 30 km south-east of Haifa, in the hills of Ephraim, at the back of Mt. Carmel. The landscape is a harsh one. The soil is severely eroded and extremely stony, and, like most of Israel, practically bare of trees. If you read the Bible, you will notice numerous references to woods and forests. In Biblical times, the land of Israel had extensive forest cover. According to some writers, quite a lot of the forest survived until something more than a century ago, when the Turks had a railway built in Palestine --- a branch line, connecting Haifa and Jerusalem to that great railroad network (stretching from Istanbul down into Arabia and Africa) which the French and the Germans built for Turkey during the nineteenth century. The wood-burning locomotives finished off whatever timber was left over from making the sleepers for the line. There is no native forest land to speak of in Israel today --- only a few pitifully small stands of trees at half a dozen locations. All the "forests" that a visitor sees, are plantations, established by Jewish enterprise during the past century.

We settled in. Zara and I had begun to suspect that she might be pregnant, and now this was confirmed. So it was decided to send her off to Ein Hashofet, a nearby *kibbutz*, where she would work part time, and learn Hebrew the rest of the day, coming home at week-ends. I was put to work in the fields of Gal-Ed. Our absorption into Israel as new immigrants and pioneers had begun.

The months at Gal-Ed gave the members of our group time to get to know each other better, before we moved to a more permanent home. During the daytime --- we worked.

The conditions weren't what we were accustomed to; mostly because of the climate. It wasn't so hard for me; I'd grown up in Chile. But for someone who'd spent their formative years on, say, Clydeside, the brilliant sunshine and burning heat of summer took a bit of getting used to. So did other things. Harvesting onions, for instance. We'd put the onions into jute bags, which were left lying in the field. Later, when you came round with tractor and trailer to pick them up, there'd be anywhere from one to half-a-dozen scorpions under each sack. They too found the sun hot, and welcomed a bit of shade; and they did not relish being disturbed. We loaded those sacks very gingerly indeed. The sting of that particular variety of scorpion is not fatal, but it can cause great pain for many hours.

Another novelty for us was the need to irrigate almost anything that grew. In England, getting the water *out* of the sodden fields is often the problem, not the reverse. At Gal-Ed, an enormous amount of time and effort was devoted to moving irrigation pipes from place to place in the fields. These pipes were of aluminium, in sections about four meters long, which could be coupled end to end, to stretch from one end of a field to the other. Some of the pipe sections had a rotating sprinkler attached to them, so when the water was turned on, it sprinkled a strip of land about eight meters wide, along the whole length of the pipe.

After a prescribed period, you turned the water off and moved the pipes down to the next strip. The only crops that grew without water were the seasonal field crops --- barley, wheat, sorghum --- which were sown in winter, and grew during the rainy season, ripening through the summer.

Dehydration is a constant danger when you're out in the open under such conditions. We learned the importance of taking plenty of water with us into the fields, and of swallowing large amounts of it regularly. Of course, there's always some fool who thinks the laws of nature don't apply to him; we learned how to revive such people, when they collapsed.

The people of Gal-Ed were agreeably surprised at our high standards of work --- our rigorous training in England now paid off. After work, in the evenings, our group activities were much more relaxed, less regimented, than they'd ever been in England. I suppose there was a feeling of "well, we finally made it" --- even though we were still a long way from settling down permanently. We were transients at Gal-Ed, and never got very involved with the life of the place. But, it gave us an idea of what life in Israel was going to be like. Israel was a very poor country, busy trying to recover from an exhausting war of independence, and to absorb a huge influx of immigrants.

Work was hard, but we were well prepared for that, and took it in our stride. The food was not meager, but boring and lacking in variety. Essential foodstuffs (meat, butter, sugar) were strictly rationed. But we could handle that, too:

even the "Tea Time" potted fish ("HERRING *and other fish*," said the label), made in England, but not on sale there. The British Ministry of Food would not pass it as fit for human consumption; but we consumed it willingly enough, regardless.

Occasional interruptions to our daily round were provided by such events as a week of intensive study of Hebrew, at a school in Jerusalem; or a day-trip to visit an exhibition called "Conquest of the Desert," also in Jerusalem. All I remember of that exhibition is lots of photographs with inspirational captions, in Hebrew and Mideast-flavoured English --- and not much else, except for a section of the concrete pipe used in the Yarkon-Negev water pipeline.

We still had lots of group discussions in our common-room at Gal-Ed. Most of them were about what we were going to do next.

~~~~~~~~~~~~~~~~~~~~~~~~~

The *kibbutz* movement with which we were affiliated --- there were several of these, separated from each other by all sorts of political and ideological distinctions (some of them so fine as to be quite incomprehensible), to which their members clung with all the irrational, intensely personal, frantic jealousy which is characteristic of Israeli politics --- wanted us to join an already established *kibbutz*, rather than to found a new one of our own. In the five years of Israel's existence, a large number of new *kibbutz*im had been started up, often from military considerations; they had an important role to play in the country's overall defense strategy, and their geographical location --- near one or other border, or in sparsely populated areas --- often reflected this. Many of these recent settlements were numerically small, and needed reinforcing --- not only in the military sense: some of them were too small to be economically or socially viable.

We were taken round the country to visit several such settlements. The *kibbutz*im we visited were clearly strapped for man- and woman-power, and we very soon saw that we were considered a pretty desirable group; we were courted assiduously wherever we went. There was a general consensus among us, that we didn't want to join any of the handful of *kibbutz*im which had already been established by previous groups of pioneers from British *Habonim*. I think there were two main reasons for this. One was that we wanted to be among people who didn't speak English.

Speaking Hebrew in Israel has always been a big thing, in the Zionist ideology we had absorbed (we'd been studying Hebrew assiduously throughout our training, and most of us had already at least a smattering), and we feared that in a *kibbutz* where most or all of the members were English-speaking, we would be more tempted to backslide.   I think, however, that a much more cogent reason for most of our group not wanting to join an "English" *kibbutz* such as Beit Ha'Emek or Kfar Hanassi, was that the members of these *kibbutz*im were on the average, several years older than ourselves, and had been senior members and youth leaders in *Habonim* in Britain, when our group had been juniors. Many of our members feared, I think, that they might find themselves being treated as juniors once more. An irrational fear, probably; yet I know it was real to many of our members.

After visits to several *kibbutz*im, and meetings with their members, we finally decided to join Amiad. This *kibbutz* had been founded about four years earlier. Some of the founders had been born in Israel; others had arrived as children before independence, and had grown up in various *kibbutz*im. During the War of Independence a number of them had been in the *Palmach*, the shock troops of the Haganah. The place where they had settled was in the hills of Northern Galilee, on the road from Tiberias up to Rosh Pina. A year or two earlier, they had been joined by a group of Dutch pioneer immigrants of the same age. Their average age was not very different from our own – maybe a year or two older. The *kibbutz* was still at the very beginning of its life. This is where our lives were going to be, and where we would play our part in rebuilding the land – the part for which we had been preparing ourselves these past few years.

In October, 1953, we departed Gal-Ed and moved to Amiad. It is in a beautiful location, in a small valley in the hills of Galilee. Looking south you can see the Sea of Galilee (Lake Kinneret) in the distance Behind the kibbutz the heights soar up and up to Tzfat (Safed). Tzfat is only 5 or 6 km away as the crow flies, but to reach it by road is about 20 km via Rosh Pina and a circuitous road through the hills. The kibbutz was very new, that was one of the things we liked about it. We didn't want to go to a place that had already been there for 30 years. At that time Amiad was called a border kibbutz; it was only 3 km from the Jordan River which was the border with Syria. That area was very sparsely populated. The nearest towns were Tiberias 30 km to the south and Rosh Pina which was a village, or *moshavah,* 5 km to the north. And in between there were just one or two kibbutzim all settled by ex-members of the *Haganah.*

Many members of Amiad had served in the *Palmach* in the War of Independence, so they were qualified fighters. The kibbutz was a part of what was called *Haganah Merhavit* --- a regional civil defense network, involving a number of similar settlements. Each kibbutz had its own armory --- I don't think we had a machine gun between us, just rifles and ammunition. At that time, we still had armed guards patrolling the kibbutz perimeter at night. All the men regularly did a stint as *shomrim.*

In November, 1953, a very short while after we moved to Amiad, the males in our group, and the unmarried females, were conscripted into the Israel Defense Forces (IDF). Military service in Israel was an education in itself. Like all educational experiences, some of it was fun, some of it was not. My *haverim* and I were infantrymen; our unit was part of an organization inside the IDF called *Nahal* (an acronym for "Fighting Pioneer Youth"). This meant that for part of our military service, we would be billeted on a border *kibbutz* (in our case, our own *kibbutz*, Amiad), training part-time, working part-time.

In each kibbutz, the army built a little army camp for its soldiers, with little wooden huts, and a clubhouse (*moadon).* We were supposed to sleep in these huts every night. We were an unusual group; most such groups were all young people of 18 or 19 years old, straight out of school, but we were older, aged up to 25 and some of us were married. In fact one of our families had a baby, a little girl. The married men among us didn't fancy sleeping in an Army hut, while our wives languished alone, a hundred yards away, in their rooms in the kibbutz. At night, we would sneak away regularly, much to the chagrin of our platoon commander, Dan, who was a bit of a pompous ass, and took his duties terribly seriously (I think he aged several years during the few months he spent with us). He would lie in ambush, and arrest us married men as we crept back to our official quarters in the small hours. Eventually, we received official permission to cohabit with our wives twice a week in our civilian homes. This affair, we later learned, was the subject of much ribald discussion at battalion headquarters.

I can't do justice here to the time I and my fellow-pioneers spent in the IDF. I wouldn't have missed it for the world. Half-way through military service, I was transferred to the Signal Corps. This was because the medical examiners, at the time of our enlistment, had classified me as being "not fully fit for combat," due to my partial deafness (the result of a childhood accident). Being unfit for combat due to impaired hearing, I was re-assigned for training..... as a wireless operator! Who can fathom the labyrinthine depths of the military mind? Fortunately, I had very acute hearing in my one undamaged ear, and completed my training as a *"morsist"* with no difficulty at all (at that time, a great part of military radio traffic was in Morse code, using WW2 surplus equipment). I never had any hearing problems as a signalman. In May 1956, I was discharged into the IDF reserves, with the honorable rank of *Tura'i* (private soldier).

My first reserve duty was in October 1956 --- "Operation Kadesh," the Sinai Campaign. I served in the Signals company of No. 9 Infantry Brigade, which was assigned to capture and occupy Sharm-el-Sheikh. It took the Brigade a week to get there travelling at a snail's pace through a dusty, trackless wilderness. I remember the delight of bathing afterwards in the waters of the Straits of

Tiran. Like other Israelis I continued to do the reserve duty for many years.

~~~~~~~~~~~~~~~~~~~~~~~~

Our eldest son Raphael was born on January 29, 1954, while I was away at training camp. Zara felt the contractions coming on one Friday morning, and asked to be driven down to the Scottish Mission Hospital in Tiberias, at that time the only lying-in hospital in all of Galilee. The hospital was half an hour's drive away. But there was no vehicle available; they were all out at work. So Zara went out to the main road to wait for a bus. While she was waiting, a car came by, and stopped to offer her a lift (people did things like that, in those days). So she hitch-hiked to hospital, and Raphael was delivered a little later that day. It was a quick and easy birth. Later that afternoon, when I arrived at the *kibbutz* for weekend leave, I was told, "you're a father."

The next five years we spent at Amiad. They were busy years. Zara eventually became *economit* ---a job she had done so well at The Grange. She did it very well here, too, doing away with a number of absurd practices which had been kept up for no other reason than "we've always done it that way."

(kibbutzniks, despite having created a revolutionary new society, could often be extremely conservative about the details of their everyday lives). One of the first things she did was to get rid of the *"metek."* This was a solution of saccharine, which we used for sweetening our tea and coffee (*matok* means "sweet" in Hebrew), sugar having been in short supply for many years. *Metek* was kept in little aluminium vessels shaped like teapots; at mealtimes, there would be one on each table, in the communal dining-room where we ate all our meals. This vile stuff was so corrosive, that within a few months it would eat holes in the metal teapots, which would have to be replaced. It was truly horrible. "We've got sugar," said Zara (rationing had begun to be a little less severe). "Let's use it." Out went the *metek,* and instead, there appeared a bowl of sugar on every table. What a relief it was, to drink a cup of tea that didn't taste like effluent water from an electrochemical plant!

Another of Zara's innovations was the introduction of breakfast cereal. Our usual breakfast fare included a sort of porridge, made from semolina. Sometimes this was edible, sometimes not, depending on who'd cooked it. One Saturday morning we came down to breakfast, and found

"Shalva" on all the tables --- puffed wheat, to be eaten with fresh milk and sugar! We gorged on it quite outrageously at first, till the novelty wore off; then it became a part of our lives.

Despite the dire predictions of pessimists (*"this will bankrupt us!"*), Zara showed that things like this could be done without bringing the *kibbutz* economy down in ruins. She was very rational about management, and had no time for what she saw as absurd preconceived notions. But one thing she couldn't do a lot about was the *halva* and *naknik.*

The founders of Amiad had grown up in Palestine in the 1930's and 40's, when times were extremely hard, and their diet, consequently, had been frugal in the extreme. Foodstuffs such as *halva,* a sweetmeat made from sesame seeds (or more commonly in our day, peanuts) and honey or sugar, and *naknik* (sausage), were enshrined in their imaginations as the height of luxury. I remember the *naknik* of those days --- we adults occasionally got a couple of slices as a treat for supper. Whatever it was made from --- a secret to which only the manufacturers, and possibly God, were privy ---, it was dyed a bright shocking pink with "edible" dyes. Now, these same founders were grown up, with children of their own, and they were determined that their children should have the luxuries which had been unavailable to themselves. So the *kibbutz* children got to eat disproportionate amounts of *naknik* and *halva*. This deeply distressed Zara, who preferred our children to be fed more mundane foods, such as the eggs, whole milk, fresh fruit and vegetables which the *kibbutz* produced in plenty.

It was things of this kind that eventually convinced Zara that *kibbutz* life was not for her. She could not bear, she said, to have her children reared by people whom she considered less competent than herself to do so.

We left the *kibbutz* after five years. Those five years, and the two years which preceded them --- the years I have written about, on the farm in England --- were, in some ways, possibly the most important years in all our lives. We learned a great deal about living and working with other people, about mutual dependence, about cooperation, about self-imposed discipline; we saw at first hand the strengths (and the fatal weaknesses) of communal, co-operative living. I wouldn't have missed those years for anything in the world. Among other things, we formed bonds of comradeship which have survived the years and the decades, and which only death can undo.

Today, the *kibbutz* ideal which we tried to live by is largely in ruins --- torn down by its own offspring, the children and grandchildren of its founders. These second and third generations of *kibbutz* children have unequivocally rejected the Utopian principles which governed the society in which they were born and raised. *Kibbutz*im have been, or are in the process of being, reorganized on strictly capitalist lines. They have been "privatized." The maxim *"from each according to his ability --- to each according to his needs"* has been replaced by the more familiar --- and more ancient --- *"to each, whatever he can wring out of the society he lives in,"* and its corollary: *"....and Devil take the hindmost."* Looking around at the society we live in today, I feel very privileged to have had a share --- however small, however fleeting --- in Utopia.

6. Leaving the *kibbutz*, making a living

I wasn't in a hurry to leave the *kibbutz*. First of all, it meant turning my back on all the socialist ideals we'd been making such a hullabaloo about these past few years, and espousing once more those bourgeois values we had rejected. This in itself was a difficult thing to do. And quite apart from that, *kibbutz* life had a lot of attractions for me. Perhaps the greatest of these was the security it offered. Out there, "In Town," was a frightening free-for-all.

My years of Army service had given me a glimpse of the way people who were on their own, had to struggle to make ends meet --- often without much success. In the *kibbutz*, I and my family were safe. All I had to do was to make my contribution, whatever it was, to the life of the *kibbutz* --- my work, my skills, whatever abilities I could call up, great or small, it didn't matter --- and I never needed to worry again about a roof over my own and my family's head, about where our next meal was to come from, about clothes and shoes and schooling for the kids, about anything. All those things were taken care of in the *kibbutz*. Outside, looking after my family would be my responsibility. I found the prospect absolutely terrifying.

Zara and I argued long about this, often bitterly. But she was determined. So when Zalman (one of the pillars of the *kibbutz*, whom we all admired) asked me if I would agree to be *kibbutz* secretary for an additional year, I told him I couldn't, because I wasn't going to be there. It was a distressing moment.

Once it was known that we were leaving, we weren't exactly the life and soul of the party. Other *chaverim* (members of the *kibbutz*) who secretly wished to leave, but didn't feel capable of doing so, looked at us with envy, and consequently with dislike. As far as the others were concerned, we were dropouts --- no longer members of the community, and therefore, no longer of much interest or importance.

We made our preparations as quickly as we could. Taking advantage of the few day's leave we had to our credit, we travelled to town to make our arrangements. I found myself a job, as tester in the chemical laboratory of the Haifa oil refinery. Zara found us a place to stay in Kiryat Tivon, near Haifa. On 29 January, 1958 (Raphael's fourth birthday), we put our meagre worldly goods on the back of a lorry, and drove out of the *kibbutz* to our new life. It was a cold winter's day, and raining. Zara and Raphael sat in the cabin with David, the driver. I sat on the back. Luckily, there was a tarpaulin over the back of the lorry, which kept some of the rain off our worldly goods and me.

~~~~~~~~~~~~~~~~~~~~~~~

In material terms, we took very little with us. Our cash allowance as kibbutz leavers was 200 lira (about 40 pounds sterling) each. We spent a good bit of this before ever leaving the kibbutz, on things we were going to need, and weren't going to get from the kibbutz: a paraffin stove for cooking, some pots and pans, some extra clothes. We still had enough left to put down a month's rent in advance (50 lira) and to feed ourselves, until I could get an advance on my pay after two weeks' work. Our furniture was the simplest: three iron beds, mattresses, and bedclothes; a table and four stools, a ramshackle two-door cupboard; a child's table and chairs for Raphael. We had the clothes we wore in the kibbutz.

Our "apartment" was in a small building in the back yard of the home of an elderly couple, Mr. and

Mrs. Zemel. There was a bedroom, a small kitchen with cold water tap and sink, and a bathroom. You got hot water in the bathroom by lighting a paraffin stove under the water tank on the wall, and waiting a couple of hours. The tank held 30 litres: enough for three showers, if you were quick. Cooking (Zara did this with extraordinary skill) was done on the same paraffin stove with which we heated water for the shower. Zara had bought a little oven-like apparatus, made of enamelled sheet metal, with a hole in the bottom which fitted over the top of the paraffin stove. In it, she used to roast and bake things. She roasted whole chickens in it, with potatoes, and onions too. Sometimes she baked a kind of biscuits she called "flapjacks," with oatmeal and honey. She had also bought something called a *"wundertopf"* --- a deep, circular aluminium pan, with a sort of chimney up the middle. With this she could bake cakes, on top of the same stove. When I got my first month's pay, we bought a second paraffin stove, and more pots and pans. After this, the cuisine in the Hurst ménage was positively Lucullan.

Looking back now, I suppose that from the standpoint of the frantic consumer society which we inhabit today, our lives were Spartan in the extreme. Our total electrical equipment consisted of two electric light bulbs, a radio, and a small fan. If we needed to travel anywhere beyond walking distance, we took a bus, like everybody else. But we didn't feel Spartan, or deprived in any way. It was a very happy time for us. Zara felt a great relief, at having left behind a society in which she no longer felt at home; and I, too, had an overpowering sense of relief, at the growing realization that the world outside the *kibbutz* was not as terrifying as it had seemed; and that I might actually be capable of coping with it, and taking care of my family, after all.

Raphael seemed to adapt well, to what we thought would have been a tremendous change for him. In the *kibbutz*, he lived apart from us, in a house with five or six other children, who ate, played, and slept together, looked after by full time care takers. He would only see us in the afternoons, after work. We would come to the children's house and collect him, bringing him back there and leaving him at bedtime. There was little to distinguish between Zara and me, from the point of view of our functional relationship with our son. In fact, until he was about three years old, he called either of us "Abba" (father) or "Ima" (mother) indiscriminately: both words meant much the same to him. Simply "parent."

207

In town, things changed very quickly. A few weeks into our new life, Zara told me this story: Raphael came up to her while she was preparing a midday meal, and said "Ima, where is Abba?" She replied: "Abba is away working, so that he can look after us all."

"Will he come back?"
"Of course, dear, he always comes back."
"But supposing something happens, and he doesn't come back?"
"Don't worry, dear, Abba *will* come back."
"Yes --- but if he doesn't, will you marry me?"

Zara found a kindergarten nearby for Raphael. It was a comfort to her to know that if she didn't like the way he was looked after, she could find him another kindergarten. We thought he might miss the company of his former roommates, and bought him a little teddy bear. He developed a strong attachment to it. It appears in several of the pictures he painted twenty years later. My grandchildren tell me he's still got it somewhere.

Months passed by. We had a visit from an old school friend of mine, Bill Gillitt. I hadn't seen Bill since he left Chile in 1945, to go to a public school in England. Later, he had studied architecture in London. He came to Israel to work for a year, in the office of an architect called Carmi, whose son had been a fellow-student. Somehow, Bill had got to hear that I was living in Israel, at Kibbutz Amiad. I received his letter a few days before we left the kibbutz, and was able to write, telling him where we would be in Haifa. A few weeks after our move, Bill showed up. We sat up in our room for hours, gleefully reminiscing. The hours passed by; it was long after midnight. But every time we suggested turning in, Bill would conjure up another episode of our schooldays, and we would relive it. He seemed almost desperate to recall the past, in ever more minute detail. Finally, at about two in the morning, I could stand no more, and got up and pulled the spare bed (which had folding legs) out from underneath ours. Bill's face lit up like a beacon. He beamed at us. "I didn't realize you had it," he said, laughing with relief. "I was terrified you were going to invite me to get into bed with you!"

Bill stayed in Israel longer than the year he'd originally planned. Carmi was a well-known architect, and gave Bill some interesting jobs. He designed a movie theatre (the "Hod" cinema in Tel Aviv), and spent several months in Jerusalem, as architect-on-site at the Knesset, the construction of which had been entrusted to Carmi's firm. He bought himself a Vespa scooter, on which he travelled the length and breadth of the country. Bill was the only person we knew in Israel who had motorized transport of his own. When he eventually left to go to America, he was married to a girl he'd met here. We have been in touch ever since; Bill came to visit Israel some years ago, with his second wife, Barbara, and spent a day with us.

After a few months in the Zemels' back yard, we were ready to move into more permanent quarters. At this point, we got lucky. We learned that, despite having already been five years in the country, the Jewish Agency was still prepared to recognize us as "new immigrants" and give us a low-interest, long-term mortgage to buy a house of our own. This special favourable treatment was accorded us because, having come from the U.K., we were "Anglo-Saxons." Immigrants from North and South America were considered "Anglo-Saxons" too, and received similar concessions. I've often wondered what motivated the Jewish Agency to treat us as special. Perhaps they thought that anybody who had come to Israel from choice, and was still here after five years, deserved to be encouraged. The long and the short of it was, that we moved into a semi-detached bungalow on the outskirts of Kiryat Atta (an outlying suburb of Haifa).

It had two rooms, a bathroom, and a kitchen, and a little plot of land --- about 200 square meters. The monthly mortgage payments were only a little more than the fifty lira we had been paying the Zemels in rent. The down payment of 1000 lira was taken care of by Zara's father. He sent us 200 pounds, which just covered it. Our house was part of a housing project for about 40 new immigrant families, called "The Marmoresh Housing Project" because it had originally been planned for immigrants from Marmoresh, or Maramuresh, which is an isolated mountain region somewhere in the Carpathian mountains. Only about five families had actually found their way from Marmoresh to Kiryat Atta; the rest of our neighbours were young, fairly recent arrivals in Israel who'd left kibbutz, like Zara and me. Two of the families were well known to us, being also late of Amiad.

Kiryat Atta was about a half-hour bus ride from downtown Haifa, and our house was the last in the street. Beyond it, human habitation ended: there began the ploughed fields of Kibbutz Ramat Yokhanan. At night, the jackals would howl in the fields ---- which I was glad of, because I'd grown used to their sound in the kibbutz, and had missed it at the Zemels' place. Now I slept more peacefully, with that doleful, oddly human-sounding wailing in my ears.

~~~~~~~~~~~~~~~~~~~~~~~~~~~~~

So there we were --- Israel householders at last. Our establishment was still pretty basic. We kept perishable foods in a wooden, zinc-lined ice-box (purchased second-hand, for twenty lira). The iceman came with his zinc-and sawdust insulated van, three times a week, and with his cleaver he would cut us a third of a block, to be carried home in a bucket.

Another regular visitor to the neighbourhood was the *neft* man. He had a horse and cart with a tank on the back, from which he would measure out ten liters of *neft* (kerosene) into our jerry-can. We used it for cooking and heating. The soda-bottle man came once a week, before the week-end. We would give him our two empty soda siphons (for which we'd paid a one-time deposit) and get two full ones. Laundry was done by hand. Food could be purchased at a variety of small neighbourhood shops --- grocer, butcher, baker, fishmonger --- within comfortable walking distance.

There may have been a supermarket somewhere in Israel at that time, but there certainly wasn't one in Kiryat Atta. Clothes, one travelled to Haifa to buy. We weren't in the market for clothes. I'd bought a tweed jacket while we were still at Amiad, to wear at job interviews. I hadn't any other use for it, really.

As always, Zara kept us well fed, despite our slender means. Soon after we left the kibbutz, I bought her a copy of a famous classic of Anglo-Jewish *belles-lettres*: "*Florence Greenberg's Cookery Book.*" Kate has it now, much thumbed and annotated. On the flyleaf is written: "For Zara. Hopefully, Elliott. 1.III.1958." Inside the back cover, I wrote an "Economy Conversion Table" for impecunious ex-*kibbutzniks*. Economy or no, we always had good food to eat, even though throughout her life, Zara scorned to keep a written household budget. "I don't need one of those," she said. "We'll always manage on whatever we've got." And she was as good as her word.

We settled in. We planted things in our yard: gladioli, strawberries, carnations. We got to know our neighbors along the street --- some of them, like the Rasnic family, have remained friends for life. Our next-door neighbors, the Lebels, were a childless couple who'd arrived from Egypt a couple of years earlier (many Jews came to Israel from Egypt, after the Sinai campaign of 1956). They both worked --- he was an engineer, she a nurse. They had no children, only a young dog called Blackie, which they left in their house during the day. Mrs. Lebel spoiled him; she used to bring him chocolate. Raphael and his friend Itzik observed this, and soon got on the chocolate bandwagon. I remember seeing them one day, standing on the neighbour's doorstep and banging on the front door, crying *"Ima shel Blackie! Ima shel Blackie! Tni lanu shokolad!"* ("Blackie's Mum! Blackie's Mum! Give us some chocolate!")

Raphael appeared to settle down comfortably. He didn't seem to miss his former way of life and companions; he had no difficulty making new friends; and there were all sorts of new experiences for him. He'd never travelled on a bus, or seen a town before, and enjoyed our occasional trips to Haifa. Raphael's first visit to the cinema was a thrilling experience. We saw "Tom Thumb" --- an enchanting movie: the comic "villains" were Peter Sellers and Terry-Thomas. We took him to the circus --- it was called the "Medrano" Circus. He still recalls some of the hilarious antics the clowns got up to. I do too --- they were brilliant. How we roared!

I worked shifts at the refinery --- four days on, one day off. It wasn't particularly demanding work. My mates were good fellows, and we got on well. We did all the routine testing of the refinery's products: Liquefied Petroleum Gas (the bottled gas used in homes), gasoline, kerosene, gasoil, light and heavy fuel oil, and asphalt. We tested the intermediate products too. After a few months, I was promoted to shift leader, and after about a year and a half on shifts, I was put in charge of the chemical testing laboratory. This was simple chemical testing, which any reasonably well-trained lab technician could have done. It was a day job; but the raise in pay compensated for the loss of my shift bonus, so we were no worse off, cash-wise.

Zara decided that the best way for her to augment our income was to give English lessons privately. Very soon after she began, Zara had as many pupils as she wanted. She was a superlative teacher. Later, when we came to live in Hadera, she got a teacher's licence, and taught in schools. Every year at the end of the school year, school principals from all the schools near Hadera would get in touch, to ask if she would come and work for them the following year.

Our material circumstances improved. Out went the icebox, to be replaced by a second-hand refrigerator: a "Western Electric" of pre-WW2 vintage. It had a door with a latch which didn't quite close: you had to jam a fork or a spoon in behind the catch. The freezer was just large enough to hold a frozen chicken, and a small ice tray. True, it sounded a bit like a motor-bike; but living with it was like living alongside the railway line --- after a while, one didn't notice the noise. And that refrigerator functioned faultlessly in our successive homes, for over ten years – no "planned obsolescence" in those far-off days. Household appliances were built to last.

The kerosene stoves were superseded, too, by a three-ring gas cooker, which stood on the marble tabletop beside the kitchen sink. The stoves were still used, for heating. I made a distributor, or diffusor, from a large tin can, so that the heat from the stove wouldn't all rise straight to the ceiling. In hardly any time after leaving the kibbutz, here we were, living like kings already.

After a few months, Zara got pregnant. She hadn't wanted to have another child while we were still in the kibbutz. With two small kids in tow, she said, she'd never have been able to get me to leave. She was probably right.

Four months or so into the pregnancy, things began to go wrong. Within a few weeks, Zara was in hospital; but nothing could be done, and she miscarried. By some unhappy mischance (I can't believe anyone could have been so callous, or so stupid, as to let her see it intentionally), Zara saw the baby's body before they took it away. "It was a little boy" she told me sadly.

Within a few months, Zara was pregnant again. This time, there were no complications: our son Dan was born on May 3rd, 1960, in the "Elisha" hospital in Haifa.

By this time we were on the move again….. I had already decided that a career in oil was not really my scene, and had started looking round for another job. In response to a newspaper ad, I put on my sports jacket and my pair of flannel trousers, and a clean shirt, combed my hair (I had quite a lot of it, then) and went for an interview at the Hadera Paper Mill. The mill had started up seven years earlier, with one paper machine. Now they'd installed a second machine, and were about to start it up, and were taking on a lot of additional personnel – including a chemist.

There were at least half-a-dozen applicants waiting for an interview, besides myself. I talked to the

Chief Chemist (he was The Only Chemist, actually, I learned later: so I immediately became no. 2, by default) and to the personnel manager, and was told "don't call us, we'll call you." A week or so later, they called me, and told me I could start work with the title of Day Shift Chemist. My salary was going to be only about 10% more than I was getting at the Refinery; but I reckoned my prospects were better. So I accepted the job, and reported for work on 1 April, 1960.

The mill was a long way from home. I had to get up at about 4:30 A.M., get a bus to Haifa, and then another bus to Hadera, to get to work by 7 A. M. After work it was the same in reverse: I'd get home at about 7 P.M. This was a difficult time for all of us; in the middle, Chaim was born. We reckoned, the sooner we moved to Hadera the better. In any case, one condition of getting the job had been that we move there.

Hadera is a small city on the Mediterranean coast of Israel, equidistant between Tel Aviv and Haifa. It was founded in 1890 as a farming colony, in an area of swamp land. The incidence of malaria was so high there that nearly half of the early colonists died. The main hospital is named after the doctor, Hillel Yaffe, who came to Hadera and worked to conquer malaria. Hadera was re-established some years later during a concerted effort to drain the swamps. Many ditches were dug and eucalyptus trees from Australia were planted, since it was believed (erroneously) that they would dry out the soil. By 1930 the population had grown to 2,000 and by 1952 to 11,800, and in 2013 the population had swelled to 90,000. It has some industry including the only large Paper Mill in Israel.

The move to Hadera wasn't easy. We had to find a place to live. We found a two-room house for rent, in a run-down neighbourhood within walking distance of the centre of town. It had been built during, or just after, Israel's War of Independence ten years earlier, and was already falling apart. And we had to sell our house in Kiryat Atta. We couldn't sell it to just anybody --- the buyer had to be someone with special immigrant's rights, like us, who would take over our mortgage. We were lucky, and found someone. So, off we were again. We still didn't have much baggage to move, fortunately.

~~~~~~~~~~~~~~~~~~~~~~~~~

When we arrived at our new home, there was a party going on in the garden next door. A little girl of about 10 came over; she told us her name was Sara, and that the party was for her brother

Moshe's bar mitzvah, and that we were invited. So we went over and met our neighbors, the Goldbergs. They were kindly people. They looked a little old to be the parents of these two children --- more like grandparents. Later we learned that mother and father had each had a spouse and children in pre-war Poland, all killed by the Nazis; only they had survived. After the war, they met in a D.P. camp, and eventually started a new life. It was only 15 years since the war's end --- you heard many such stories in Israel.

For two years we lived in that house. Things went well for us, in a quiet way. The chief chemist, my boss, insisted that I call him "Mr. Shapiro," while he addressed me as "Mr. Hurst." This might sound commonplace enough to an Englishman, but it's not all that usual in Israel, where first names are used a great deal of the time. We got on very well. After a year or so, he said to me: "Why don't you call me Daniel, and I'll call you Elliott." He had a remarkable mind, and I learned a great deal from him. I became "Assistant Chief Chemist" as our department expanded. We took on additional professionals, and undertook some applied R&D. My salary increased considerably. Zara acquired a following of private pupils – she was never short of them. One of them, a boy called Uzzi, paid off in a wholly unexpected way, as I shall tell in a moment.

We decided that we could afford to think about owning a home of our own. After some inquiries, we put our names down for a Government housing scheme for young families. What happened from then on taught us a great deal about the way things in our country (and, I think, in most countries) sometimes happen "behind the scenes."

During our first two years in Hadera, Zara and I and the boys lived in a rented house in a neighbourhood of one-story homes that were jerry-built even by the standards of 1950. If there'd been more than one story, we'd have lived in fear of the whole house collapsing. In the living room (which doubled as our bedroom --- the other room was the boys' room) you could tell the weather outside, by looking through the cracks in the wall. When it rained, you needn't look --- the rain came in!

~~~~~~~~~~~~~~~~~~~~~~~

Anyway, we lived happily enough in this broken-down place for two years. I passed my trial period at the Paper Mill, and was accepted as a "permanent" employee. This was a status that all salaried employees hoped for, since it was very difficult for an employer to sack you, once you had *"kvi'ut,"* or tenure (even if you'd burned the company premises down, or publicly assaulted the boss, he could still have a hard time getting rid of you). Zara started giving private English lessons. She was superlatively good at this. Word quickly got round, and she was soon turning aspiring pupils away. Our combined earning power was good enough, and our prospects for the future bright enough, for us to think of bettering our living conditions. We started looking round.

Something soon turned up. A Government housing company was building a three-story, 24-family apartment building at a convenient site, 15 minutes' walk from the centre of town. We applied to the local Labour Council headquarters (the *Histadrut*, or General Federation of Trade Unions, was involved in sponsoring this project), were found eligible, got our names on to the list of candidates, and waited for the building to be finished. The apartments would be allocated by lot, at a public drawing in which all the candidates would participate.

One of Zara's pupils was a boy called Uzi. Uzi was far from stupid, but the Israel educational system had more or less bounced off him, like the proverbial water off a duck's back. He had failed his *"Bagrut"* (Matriculation certificate) exam three times in English. Certificates and documents attesting your level of education are very important in Israel. They open innumerable doors to employment opportunities which would otherwise remain closed, regardless of any personal qualities or abilities you might, or might not, possess.

Uzi's father happened to be a wealthy and influential citizen of Hadera, and Uzi's future was in no way in jeopardy from his having failed the exam. He would in time take over his father's business interests. But there was a matter of prestige involved, as well. Possession of a *"Bagrut"* certificate carried considerable cachet --- and the children of far lesser persons than Mr O. had them; a most uncomfortable situation.

After a few months' tuition from Zara, Uzi passed his English exam with flying colours. His father was overjoyed.
"What can I do for you? What do you want?" he said to Zara. "I want to do something for you."
"Thank you," she replied. "I've got everything I want."
This may have been something of an exaggeration; but it was what she said.

"Didn't you tell me you've applied to buy an apartment in a Labour Council housing project?"
"Yes."
"Where is it? Is there any particular apartment you would especially like to have?"
"Well, yes," said Zara, "there is: the top floor apartment on the Western end of the building. But the apartments will be allocated by lot, and we'll be lucky if we get one at all. There are a lot of people on the list."

A short time later the date of the draw was announced. I wasn't able to get away from work; Zara represented us. The public draw was held on the premises of the Hadera branch of the General Federation of Labour, in the presence of such dignitaries as the Secretary of the Hadera Labour Council, members of the Hadera City Council, and the Area Manager of *Shikun Ovdim*, the Government Housing Corporation in charge of the project. All, or most, of the families participating (more than 50) were present. The names of the lucky (or unlucky --- who knew?) ones were on folded slips of paper in a glass bowl, to be picked out at random by an Impartial Official, in clear view there of all.

The draw began. "Apartment no. 1" intoned the clerk from his list. The Impartial Official stepped forward, put his hand in the bowl, and took out a slip of paper. "Family Schuster" he read. And so it went on. Finally, the clerk read out "Apartment number 18." This was the coveted top floor apartment at the Western end of the building. The Impartial Official put his hand into the bowl. "Family Hurst" he proclaimed. We were in --- lucky, lucky us!

Israel has all kinds of lotteries. Many Israelis love to gamble. There are lotteries for the Anti-Cancer Fund, for the Soldier's Welfare Committee. Zara and I always used to buy tickets for the Soldiers' Welfare Committee lottery. There were valuable prizes: apartments, cars. Tax-free, if you won one. One day Zara saw me tearing up some pieces of paper.

"What are you tearing up?" She took a closer look. "Aren't these tickets for the Soldiers' lottery?"

"Yes."

"But the draw's not for another two weeks! Why are you tearing them up?" Well, I said, the Soldiers' Welfare Committee had already got our money, which was after all, the idea behind the lottery; eventually, some army camp would get a TV set, or a coffee-making machine, a little piece of which would have been paid for out of our contribution. "But we can't win anything if you tear the tickets up!" No, I said, I suppose not. We didn't see eye to eye about this. She never let me buy tickets again. I don't know if she ever bought them without letting me know --- I doubt it.

Years later, after Zara's death, a law was passed requiring institutions to publish the salaries paid to their top officials. In this way I learned that the General Manager --- or whatever the head honcho is called --- of the Soldier's Welfare Association, was paid a salary equal to approximately eight times what I was earning as Chief Chemist, at the time of my retirement from the Paper Mill. That's beside his expense account, and the official car. I'm not sure whether to be glad or sorry that Zara never knew this.

We have a football pool in Israel, too. It's immensely popular. It is nominally under the control of the Minister of Education, Culture and Sport, but in fact it's farmed out to private "entrepreneurs." A few years ago, the State Controller's Annual Report had a detailed account of these racketeers, and of the jiggery-pokery they are up to --- or at any rate, were up to at that time. Maybe someone else is running the pools now;

after all, someone else is Minister. *"Plus ça change,"* wrote some wise Frenchman, *"plus c'est la même chose."*

Then we have *Mifal Hapayis* --- the State Lottery. Millions and millions of shekels are paid out every month. There's a public drawing on TV, with neon lights flashing, and fluorescent coloured balls leaping about inside a glass sphere, transparent, for all to see (and of course, half-naked, pneumatic young ladies all around). Actually, the *Mifal Hapayis* Corporation operates all kinds of draws and lotteries. There are prizes galore for the fortunate winners. A few months ago, I read in my wife's newspaper that the Director-General of *Mifal Hapayis* had taken home a car that he'd won in the lottery (we were told later that after the public fuss following the newspaper report, he had given the keys back, and presumably the car as well). The newspaper article said also that the previous year, it had been the Deputy Director-General's turn, and he (lucky man!) had taken a car home as a prize, too .

In Israel, employees of the lottery are allowed to take part in the draw. In most countries, they're not. There are so many tempting ways, after all, of fiddling the results. All tickets, whether sold or not, participate in the draw --- and what could be easier, for someone on the inside, than to purchase, after the event, winning tickets which weren't sold, and to juggle the books pre-dating the purchase to make things look kosher? All that's necessary is for everybody who's in on the game, to keep quiet. The names of winners are not, after all, published. Of course, if the cleaning lady who was told she'd win a refrigerator, gets a mere toaster oven instead, she may be tempted to leak the story to the papers, just out of spite (I know I would be).

My second wife Kate has an annual subscription to *Mifal Hapayis*. It's only a small sum weekly, but there are several million others like her. I don't buy tickets. You may think I'm cynical about lotteries. Well……. call it sceptical.   I am old-fashioned enough to believe that lotteries ought to be won more by luck than good management – or by any kind of management, good, bad, or indifferent.

~~~~~~~~~~~~~~~~~~~~~~~~

We moved into our new apartment. It had two bedrooms, a bathroom, a kitchen, and a living room with a small balcony. From the balcony you could look westward and catch a glimpse of the Mediterranean sea; then, if you looked to the East, you could see the hills of Samaria, in what was then

Jordan. We were in the narrowest part of Israel ---
the distance from the seashore to the Jordanian
border was about 10 km. And we were in the
highest part of Hadera, too. Just a couple of
hundred meters up the road was the city's water
tower, all of fifty meters above sea level. Zara had
chosen wisely: we had fresh air from three sides.
The climb up three flights of stairs was no great
effort for any of us, not even for Chaim, who was
now two years old. There were six families to each
stairwell, two on each floor. Our neighbours were
mostly young families like ourselves, with children
the same ages as ours. Raphael and Chaim soon
found friends among them.

After two years' work at the Paper Mill I was
offered a personal contract. Until that time I had
been a "monthly employee," which mean that I was
a party to the collective agreement between the
staff, the mill, and the General Federation of
Labour. If I signed the personal contract they
offered me, I became a "manager."   No union
protection, no collective bargaining - no permanent
status. No extra pay for overtime. They could sack
me at any time. The benefits? A whopping salary
increase --- from 550 to 800 lira a month; a
telephone, paid for by the mill; free meals in the
company dining room.; a loan to buy a car, and a

120-lira-a-month tax-free allowance to go with it. And participation in the Managers' Profit-sharing Scheme, which meant about 2 month's additional pay a year, tax-free. I told Zara about the offer. We discussed it for about five seconds. I signed the contract, thinking of a song we used to sing in England years ago, to the tune of the Labour Party's anthem, "*The Red Flag*."

"The people's flag is turning pink,
It's not so red as I used to think.....
.....The working class can kiss my arse --
I've got a foreman's job at last!"

We were coming up in the world.

~~~~~~~~~~~~~~~~~~~~~~~~~~~~

We bought our first car. It was a Ford Anglia, vintage 1947 – a small black-and chromium creature, rather like a perambulator, though perhaps just a little bit larger. I remember how Mr. Klein, the garage proprietor, screamed and tore his hair when I brought it in, and asked him to get it fixed up for its annual test (he did the job, nevertheless). We were very proud of it. Not very many people had cars in Israel in those days --- which was just as well, because there weren't many roads, either; most of the roads were ones that the British had left behind, or the Turks before them.

We began to get to know our country. We joined the Israel Camping Association, which had about 15 camping sites all over the country, from Dan to Eilat. We bought a big tent with room for the four of us; and during our vacations, in the following dozen or so years when the boys were growing up, we travelled just about every road in Israel, and stayed at every single camp site in the country, at one time or another.

We didn't last long in our "lucky" apartment. There were 23 other families living in the same house. Now in Israel, if you put 24 families together, there's going to be at least one nut case among the lot, and quite possibly several more. That's a statistical fact. And these individuals do all they can to make life hell for everyone around them, with scenes, and screams, and occasional visits from the police --- you name it. We had a couple of characters of this sort among our neighbours, and after two years Zara said: "Enough. We're getting out of here. Who needs this kind of neighbours? And in any case, I don't want my kids to grow up playing in the street with *meshugganehs*. We need a house with a yard."

We found a house in a run-down, out-of-the-way neighbourhood at the southern end of Hadera. It was the only kind of neighbourhood we could afford. The "*Meckler*," or house agent, was a shoemaker, who had a shop at the back of the city market. He was good at mending shoes, and also at buying and selling homes. Nowadays --- in Hadera and everywhere else --- you can find lots of offices with signs, saying things like "Estate Agent" or "Investment Advisor." The people inside usually know nothing about mending shoes, nor about investments, nor about buying and selling houses, either. Times change.

As we walked along the main street of the neighborhood (a strip of asphalt just wide enough for a bus, with dust on either side --- no kerbs or pavements), people came out of their houses and stopped us. They knew who the shoemaker was, and what he was about. "Do you want to buy a house? Come in and look at ours!" There was a lot of building of apartments going on at that time in the center of Hadera, and people wanted to move away from this outlying neighborhood, to somewhere nearer the middle of town. So we had lots of places to choose from.

Zara finally decided on a place. It was nicely situated, on the main street of the neighborhood, with a kindergarten and a primary school close by. Anybody who's visited us in Israel knows it -- it's the same house that Kate and I live in now, 47 years later. We did all that was necessary: found a buyer for our apartment, borrowed some more money, and moved.

~~~~~~~~~~~~~~~~~~~~~~~~~~

Now I have to tell about something unhappy.

I've told our story so far in simple words, and it may sound as though things ran smoothly for us all the time; but the fact is, that they didn't. There were all kinds of stresses and strains upon both of us: and eventually --- something gave way.

I had a love affair with another woman. It got serious. Zara and I were separated for the best part of a year. Eventually, we got together again, thank goodness. If it had been otherwise, I doubt if either of us would have known much, if any, real happiness all the rest of our lives.

For the children, that time was extremely painful. They have never forgotten it, and though we don't often mention it, once in a while one of them (usually it's Chaim; Raphael's more reserved) says something that reminds me of that time, and of how deeply they suffered. They weren't the only ones. Zara was devastated; but characteristically, she took whatever steps she thought necessary for getting on with her life (including, she told me later, taking the measure of one or two other men). And she had no notion of making things easy for me, either. Quite the contrary. If I was going to walk out on her and the kids, I certainly wasn't going to get any understanding, or cooperation, from her. As far as she was concerned, all I had coming to me was a hard time. She did her best to give me one; and Zara's best was very, very good.

We got together again after about a year. If I were a believing man, I'd thank Heaven for that. And during all the rest of our life together, Zara never once reproached me for having left her and the children. *Never*. Not a single word – even when we quarrelled, as we occasionally did. For this I honour her beyond measure. Many years later, a few months before her death, Zara asked me about my former lover. She was dead, I said. "Did you go to her funeral?" she asked me. "Yes" I said. That was all.

~~~~~~~~~~~~~~~~~~~~~~~~~~

No more moves --- no more job changes --- no more family upheavals. We finally settled down. We were living within our income, and (for Israel) not badly off; we had a home and a car. Our only debts had to do with the various loans we were paying off on the house. They weren't an unbearable burden. The kindergarten, and the school, two minutes' walk up the road, turned out to be excellent: the kids loved them. We hadn't always been so lucky. A few years earlier, in Kiryat Atta, when Raphael was four years old, he showed interest in learning to read. We told his kindergarten teacher about our intention of teaching him to read. She was horrified. "Don't even think of it! If he starts school already knowing how to read, there'll be nothing for him to do! He'll go crazy with boredom! It'll be a tragedy!"

The tragedy was that we listened to this benighted fool, and refrained from teaching Raphael to read. When he started school at age six, the Ministry of Education had introduced a system of teaching children to read Hebrew, which had been devised in America for teaching people to read non-phonetic languages (the Americans had, meanwhile, already discarded the system as useless). Hebrew is written with a phonetic alphabet. It has 22 characters, which any normal, un-brainwashed child can learn to recognize after a few hours' study. The system by which Raphael was taught may have been great for learning to read Chinese, or Egyptian hieroglyphs. It was not good for learning Hebrew.

After a year at school, Raphael was still illiterate. He could recognize a few words by sight, but confused words which looked similar in print (like "shalom" and "shalem"). And what was worse --- reading lessons, with their endless repetition of the same few words, had become not merely a bore, but an affliction, to be looked forward to not with pleasure, but with dread. In the end, it took him three years to learn to read --- and he did it himself, outside of school. Even now, the recollection of this episode brings back to me an echo of the anguish we all felt.

This taught us to be very wary of anyone calling themselves an "educator." I would put most "educators" on a par with graphologists, or with people who have studied psychology by correspondence. When Chaim was about three or four, and showed an interest in learning to read, we consulted nobody, and taught him in no time at all. While still in kindergarten, Chaim would visit the Hadera children's library every Monday and Thursday, and withdraw three books (the regulation maximum) each time, returning the previous three, thoroughly read and re-read. Later, at school, he never suffered a moment's boredom --

unlike Raphael, he actually enjoyed going to school.

Many teachers in Israel aren't up to much. It's not surprising --- it's the worst paid of all professions. Almost all school teachers are women – men won't become teachers, because it's so hard to earn enough to support a family. Almost all of the very few male schoolteachers I've known, have held down two, or even three, jobs at a time, in order to make ends meet. And as incomes, and material standards, rise in Israel, so teachers get left farther and farther behind. Meanwhile, everyone complains that education is going to the dogs. I suspect it's the same everywhere.

Our lives were full of activity. We made friends --- among them, the Levy family. Victor and Ida had come to Israel from the USA. Like ourselves, they'd been kibbutzniks for a few years, then left. They both worked as schoolteachers in high schools around Hadera. Their children were the same age as ours, and we had many happy times together. And with a car, most of our friends in other parts of the country were within visiting distance. We tried to make friends with some local, Israeli-born couples, too. These friendships didn't ever get very far. Every time we found ourselves in a gathering with four or five couples of native Israelis, the gathering would quickly polarize into two groups:

the men in one corner, talking about money; the women in another, talking about children. I'm sure not all Israelis were, or are, like that. But the ones we knew in Hadera were. Boring as hell. Most of our friends ended up being people who'd come from English-speaking countries.

Zara and I were almost the only members of our respective families to come and settle in Israel. There were some distant cousins who had been here many years. Then Zara 's uncle, Lewis, and his wife Hannah, came to live in Israel during the fifties, when Lewis retired; their daughter Malka came with them, and we were in regular contact with them. All the more so, when Malka married Al and they had a boy of Chaim's age.   But Zara believed that children were entitled to have uncles, aunts, cousins galore --- most of our kids' friends had these; she thought our children were deprived in this respect.

The moment we thought Raphael was old enough (he was about 15), we packed him off to England to spend the summer visiting his relatives, Jewish and Christian alike. He loved it. I wrote to my Aunt Beatrice, apologizing for him: "he doesn't know a word of English, I'm afraid --- we've only spoken Hebrew to him, all his life." She wrote back: "What d'you mean, he doesn't speak a word of English?

He speaks it fluently. Not only that --- he has a very colourful vocabulary, too!!!" He'd been listening, all those years, to Zara and myself conversing in English, as we habitually did between ourselves. And he hadn't missed a single four-letter word. He simply assumed that – since we used them so casually -- such words were part of ordinary polite discourse, and used them so. When he came back after several weeks, we went to meet him at the airport, taking his bosom pal, Yankele. Raphael came out and greeted us in English, and went on talking volubly in that language --- even to poor Yankele, who was utterly at a loss. It was several days before Raphael managed to get back to speaking Hebrew at all. And ever since that time, he's been equally at ease speaking to us in either language.

The same thing happened five years later with Chaim. After a few weeks with the Mischofs, he came back speaking fluent English, but sounding like a cross between Sammy Mischof and Harry Lauder (*"aye, weel; a doon't knoow"*) --- something which he's never quite lost.

We began having visitors from abroad. Zara 's father Sam, had of course always been a fairly frequent visitor, coming every year or two to stay for a couple of weeks. He didn't think much of

Hadera. A hick town --- nothing happening. After a few days, he'd go off to stay at a hotel in Tel Aviv. He loved chatting up the girls along the Tel Aviv marina. He came regularly to visit, until he was well into his nineties.

Now other members of the family started coming. Rosanne was the first. She was grown up, and independent. Part of the time she stayed with us; part of the time she travelled around on her own. We took her to the Dead Sea, to Massada and Ein Gedi, where we camped. Then Rosanne's brother Stuart came. He was a medical student. We took him camping to Tel Dan, in northern Galilee, just a kilometer or two from the Syrian border (this was very shortly before the Six Day War). One balmy evening, we were eating supper on the grass outside our tent, when we heard: rat-tat-tat. Rat-tat-tat.

We took no notice, and went on eating --- but Stuart froze. *"What was that?"* Machine gun fire, we said. This place is very near the border. *"Has fighting started? What's going on?"* Nothing special, we said. Patrols are moving along the border all the time. The boys may have heard some Arab farmer's stray donkey in the bushes, and blown the poor creature away. Or they may just have been bored, and made a little *"Chicago"* for fun. Or they may have come across an infiltrator or two. We went on with our meal --- all except for poor Stuart, whose face had turned chalky white in the lamplight. He couldn't eat another mouthful. I don't think he'd ever heard a shot fired in his life, until that moment.

~~~~~~~~~~~~~~~~~~~~~~~

When Rafi was about 17, sometime in 1971, he said: "I'm not going back to school." He didn't say "I don't want to go back to school." He said "*I'm not going.*" He'd never been happy or comfortable at school, except for a few years at the primary school just up the road from our house. He'd tried several secondary schools. He found it hard to respect his teachers. "They don't want to help me learn, or to have thoughts of my own" he said. "They just want to make me think what they think."

We tried to reason with him --- to no avail. It was clear that he meant what he said.

"*So what will you do?* "
"I think I'll go away for a while."

We were distraught. What we decided to do was to stop trying to make him change his mind, and simply to tell him that he should feel free to do as he liked, only to remember that here he had a home waiting for him, and a family that loved him whatever happened. We didn't want him to cut himself off from us, we said. And if he found himself in any sort of trouble, and needed help --- he knew where we were, and should not hesitate to call on us. And we asked him please to keep in touch --- even if only to phone and say "hello, I'm still around" once in a while.

He went off --- became a wanderer, a vagrant. He lived for weeks under the arches of the aqueduct at Caesarea. He washed dishes for the restaurants there, and they gave him food. He went down to Eilat, and lived there for months, occasionally doing casual labour at the docks, sleeping on the sands at Taba; drinking the dregs from the stacks of empty bottles piled outside the back doors of restaurants, when he was down and out and thirsty. He spent weeks painting the inside of Kibbutz Yotvata's new restaurant. It was a huge job --- he developed *epicondylitis* ("tennis elbow") from so much wielding of the brush.

Every few weeks we'd get a phone call: "Hello, this is Rafi. I'm fine. How's everybody?" Very occasionally, he'd drop by, and maybe stay for a day or two. Once he showed up wearing nothing but a pair of filthy slacks, that looked as though they'd come out of a dustbin. --- "Where did you get those, for heaven's sake?" "Out of a dustbin." He'd woken up one morning on the beach at Taba (a few miles south of Eilat, in Northern Sinai), where he'd been sleeping with all his worldly goods (his clothes, his wallet, and the painting materials he always carried with him) under his head, to find that somebody had taken everything during the night, leaving him with nothing but the underpants he'd slept in. He'd found these trousers somewhere, and hitch-hiked home. I don't think he'd eaten for days. He stayed long enough to get a bath, put on clean clothes, eat some food, rest for a day or so --- and was off again.

Being a vagrant in summer is one thing --- having no home in winter is another. Yehudah, the headmaster of the 'Iron agricultural school at which Zara taught, had heard from Zara about what was happening. He said to Zara: "Tell Raphael that if he wants to come here, nobody will bother him, or ask him to do anything he doesn't want to. All we ask is that he doesn't interfere with anyone else's work." We passed the message on to Rafi. "Just think about it. No hurry." After a few days, Rafi said to his mother: "All right. I'll try it."

Nobody knows whether they're suited to a vagrant's life until they've had a serious shot at it.

Read George Orwell's description of the life of a vagrant in Europe (*"Down and Out in Paris and London"*). It's horrible: squalid, filthy, hungry. You're at the mercy of the elements --- and worse, of an inimical society. Maybe in Tahiti, it's different. But I doubt it.

Rafi enrolled at the *'Iron* school. He bothered nobody. Nobody bothered him. After a year, on his own initiative, he took the Israel Matriculation exams, and passed most of them. He stayed at the school until he was called up for military service. Yehuda and his staff earned the lifelong gratitude of Zara and myself.

~~~~~~~~~~~~~~~~~~~~~~~~~

I became interested in ancient coins through a very dear friend of mine called Jeffrey Close, since deceased.   I'd known him since before coming on *aliyah* ... he was also on *hachsharah* with *Habonim*, but in a different group from the one that we were in. Every now and then we'd have a *kenes*, a meeting of the members of the different *hachsharot*, and I remember meeting Jeffrey there with his wife.   They came to a different kibbutz, Beit Haemek, near Akko.

Jeff's wife got polio and died a year after arriving in Israel. Polio was rife in the country at that time, it was endemic. I remember when the first polio vaccine came out in 1955, it was very scarce. The first people inoculated in Israel with anti-polio serum were children up to the age of 7, and adult immigrants from the UK and the US.

The automatic assumption made by the adults that weren't vaccinated was that we were getting special privileges as Western immigrants. The fact is that polio attacks the lowest age groups, which is why it's called infantile paralysis; but when it's been present in a country for a couple of generations the age of vulnerability gradually increases. Polio has been known in the UK since early in the 19th century (I think it started in some out of the way place like St. Helena, which is a little island in the middle of nowhere). The first people to get it were British citizens, so the sickness has been present in Britain for 150 years, whereas in other countries it spread much later. When it first reaches any other country it attacks only infants at first; then the age of vulnerability creeps up, the threshold rising all the time. Jeffrey's wife came to Israel contracted polio and was dead in three days.

In Israel in 1955, hundreds of people developed polio. At Amiad one of our *chaverim*, Derek, got it and it left him paraplegic. I visited him while he was undergoing rehabilitation: he was in a swimming pool, surrounded by dozens of small children. The only other adults present were the hospital staff.

After Jeffrey's wife's death he came to Amiad where he eventually married one of the bachelor girls in our group. They left the kibbutz in 1957, a few months before I and Zara did the same.

Back to ancient coins: before coming to Israel, Jeffrey had been studying chemistry in England, but had left his studies before completing his degree. After leaving the kibbutz, he got a job at the Haifa Technion (more grandiloquently known as the Israel Institute of Technology), as a laboratory technician; at the same time, they let him study for a degree. He worked hard, and after 4 or 5 years he qualified as a chemical engineer. He continued to work at the Technion, in the Department of Environmental Engineering. His job allowed him to travel around the country, collecting all kinds of samples of water, which he and others would later analyze in the laboratory of his department. Every so often, his work would bring him to the vicinity of Hadera. When this happened, he would go off into the sand dunes around Caesarea Maritima, an ancient city whose ruins are just a few kilometers from Hadera. 50 years ago, the site was much less developed than now, with no fences, ticket offices, or rich people's luxury villas. I asked him "what are you doing out there?" He said "I'm looking for things. There's all kinds of ancient stuff on the sand there, waiting to be picked up." He showed me what he was talking about: bits of bronze, coins, fish-hooks, fragments of ancient pottery and glassware, all sorts of little bits and pieces of the city's ancient past.

History has always interested me, so I said "can I come with you?" And he said "yes." So I took off work for an hour or two, and joined him. I was lucky to be able to do this: this was my "golden age" in the late 1960's, when I had a senior position in a well-run organization,, and could take off for a couple of hours during the day without my department falling to pieces.

After that, Jeffrey would give me a phone call now and then, saying "I'm coming down to Caesarea," and we would meet and go out on the sands for an hour or two. Once I'd found a few ancient objects, I was hooked. At first, I picked up everything I found; nine-tenths of it was just fragments, but there were coins, and little implements, such as nails, pins and cosmetic instruments, and (very occasionally) an engraved gem fallen from an ancient ring, or a broken fragment of gold jewelry.

It's a very addictive occupation. It was so for me, at any rate. I got into the habit of going out every Friday afternoon (we worked Friday mornings; the five-day week was still years away), and scouring the dunes. I met other people similarly addicted: I learned that some of them had been doing this for many years, even before WW II.

We searched using nothing but our eyes. The rules were simple; they'd been laid down by the Antiquities Authority, during the British Mandate. Officially defined archaeological sites were forbidden to us: but we were legally free to range the dunes and fields for miles around the ruins, and pick up whatever we saw. Nobody bothered us. Nine-tenths of the stuff we picked up was just rubbish, scrap metal: iron, lead and bronze. But twice, I found single gold coins in the sand. Both of them were Arabic. I remember coming home with one. It was one-third of a dinar, 11th century. I showed it to the boys. Raphael, who must have been about eight years old, got so excited that he rushed out into the street, shouting "My daddy's found a gold coin! My daddy's found a gold coin!" I had it for many years, until I exchanged it in order to follow my particular interests; I eventually focused on the study of ancient weights, for which I exchanged almost everything else I had. But I kept, and still possess, a Roman ring-gem, with figures engraved on it.

Then the metal detectors arrived, and everything changed. Metal detectors meant that seekers on the dunes didn't use their eyes as much as before: most of one's time was spent listening for the *beep,* that told one there was something interesting, a few centimeters below the surface.   Jeffrey and I both acquired metal detectors, and so did everyone else who searched the sands; and our yield of ancient metal objects increased considerably. But then the robbing started. All sorts of people began sneaking into archaeological sites with metal detectors, when no-one was working at them, and digging them over. Robbers organized in gangs, and began looting archaeological sites all over the country, on a big scale, using advanced electronic detection equipment.

The Antiquities Authority was not slow to respond, with a series of Draconian laws. The whole country was declared, in effect, one big archaeological site, off-limits to all but licensed archaeologists.   Any ancient object, wherever found, was from now on state property, to be handed over to the Authority. To keep anything at all was a criminal offense, punishable by a heavy fine and even imprisonment. Jeff and I, and other amateurs like us, never looted archaeological sites: our hunting-grounds were dunes and fields, places where no archaeologist would dream of going! But there was nothing for us to do but give up. We weren't always, however, in a sufficiently great hurry to do so; a few months after the laws were passed, I was arrested --- caught with my metal detector *in flagrante delicto*, in the middle of a ploughed field, by an antiquities inspector and a Police sergeant. They took my particulars, and told me to report to the police station the following day. There, my fingerprints were taken; and a few months later, I received notice that they had filed a complaint, charging me with antiquities robbery.

I got myself a lawyer, and eventually was summoned to receive my official "Antiquities Robber's Certificate" at the Hadera Magistrate's Court. The Judge laughed at this case. He said "I'm not going to pronounce sentence on you, because that will give you a criminal record, and I don't see you as a criminal particularly. I'll put you on probation." So for the next six months I had to report, every two weeks, to the local probation officer. The only probation officer in Hadera turned out to be a *juvenile* probation officer, a young woman the age of my children. I'd sit in her anteroom, waiting for my bi-weekly interview, along with half a dozen delinquent school kids; I was the only adult. We became good friends. She was a very pleasant young woman. But I stopped looking for antiquities at Caesarea; if they had caught me a second time, I'd have got it harder. As it was, by far my severest punishment was the lawyer's fee.

~~~~~~~~~~~~~~~~~~~~~~~~~~

I had become thoroughly involved with ancient coin collecting. I bought, and studied, books about ancient numismatics, modern numismatics, and history too, and joined the Israel Numismatic Society. And I made friends with a lot of people. One of the people I made friends with was Kate's then-husband, who was at that time a recent immigrant to Israel. He'd been a coin collector in South America, where he had amassed a valuable collection of Chilean coins. This was sold at auction in the United States, and helped to finance their *aliyah*.

When he came to Israel, and started to take an interest in ancient coins, he heard that there was "this person in Hadera who collects coins, who speaks Spanish and is from Chile." So I got a phone call one day from the gate at the Paper Mill, saying "there's a gentleman here to see you." I asked his name: it was Anselmo. He explained that he had heard about me from a doctor at Hillel Yaffe Hospital. It's a small world. So we became friends.

Anselmo didn't come to Caesarea to get coins. He had different techniques from me: he liked to buy from other people. He managed to get in touch with an Arab fisherman, a diver, who used to dive and pick up stuff on the sea bottom. There are hundreds of ancient shipwrecks, all along the coast of Israel. A diver in a few meters of water can find a shipwreck, and pick up all kinds of things. It's monitored very carefully now, and there's very little an independent person can do, but at that time nobody bothered such people. He used to bring up all kinds of stuff from the sea bottom, coins, jewelry, statues, daggers. So Anselmo and I became friends, and Zara and I got to know Kate.

Things weren't going well for me at the Paper Mill. I've usually found it easier to get on with my mates, and my subordinates, than with my bosses. Without going into details, let's just say that I had succeeded in earning the dislike and distrust of a very senior person (this individual also scuttled the career of my mentor, Daniel, who by this time had left the mill). I was passed over for promotion, and eventually found myself in a very uncomfortable position: taking orders from people I neither respected nor trusted, and with little prospect of change.

I should have left at this point, but I was mortgaged. "He that hath wife and children," wrote Francis Bacon, "hath given hostages to Fortune." With one son in the army, and another in high school, I wasn't in a position to indulge my inclinations; I was defenseless. I couldn't leave. I stuck it out for two years --- then, one day, Anselmo said to me, "I've left my job; I can't stand it anymore. I want to start in business. I'm looking for a partner."

This was not long after the Yom Kippur war of 1973. The whole country was severely traumatized --- and my family was no exception. Our elder son had been wounded during the fighting (fortunately for him, as it transpired; by the time the fighting ended, more than half of the men in his armored unit were dead). Zara had left her teaching job, and gone into business as a bookseller. She said to me: "anybody who goes on teaching school past the age of fifty, is bound to lose their mind to some degree." We talked about it, not at any great length. I left the Paper Mill fairly gracefully, without quarrelling with anyone, took all my severance pay and my accumulated retirement and pension funds, and invested them in a business --- which failed.

Anselmo and I between us knew a great deal about coins. But we knew nothing about business. Dealing in coins is a business, just like any other. The principle is: buy cheap, and sell dear. The difference determines how much you can prosper. We didn't buy cheap enough, and we didn't sell dear enough. In addition, we were under-capitalized: we should have had five times the money we did.   There were a lot of opportunities we had to pass up.

Here are some examples from our short time in the coin business. My partner was away, and I was alone in the office when a young man walked in.
"What will you give me for this?" He put a coin on the table, a silver *tetradrachm* of Alexander the Great.
"Sorry, I don't want to buy it."
"Why not? Is it a fake?"
"No, it's a perfectly genuine coin. But it's quite severely worn. I don't think any of my customers would want a coin in this condition, so I'd have no-one to sell it to."
"Isn't it worth anything, then?"
"Of course it's worth something, but I don't want

it."

"Who will buy it from me, then?"

"There's a fellow with a shop at the Central Bus Station, who buys and sells all sorts of stuff --- stamps, antiques, coins. Try him."

"How much should I ask for it?"

"Ask for five hundred lira. If he haggles, settle for four. Don't take less."

"Thank you." He took his coin and went out.

A few months later, the same young man came into the shop. He walked over to my desk and put a coin on the table. It was, once again, a *tetradrachm* of Alexander the Great --- this time, in very fine condition. A handsome piece.

"Remember me?"

"Of course."

"Will you buy this from me?"

"Oh, yes. It's a very nice coin."

"What will you give me for it?"

"A thousand lira."

"Take it --- it's yours."

Then he told me the rest of the story. Before coming to me with the previous coin, he'd gone to Mr. Shaffer, a well-known dealer in stamps and coins, whose shop was not far from ours. Shaffer had been in business for many years, and had a reputation for being straight as a die. Shaffer looked at his worn tetradrachm and said: "This is rubbish. I'll give you thirty lira for it."

"Won't you give me fifty? --- forty?"

"I said thirty lira, and that's exactly what I meant. Not a *grush* more."

So the young man decided that before he sold his rubbish for thirty lira, he'd try his luck with us. After his talk with me, he ended up selling his worn tetradrachm to the man at the Central Bus station, for 450 lira. "From now on" he said, "I'll know where to sell any more coins that come my way; I know you'll offer me a reasonable price."

Mr. Shaffer died a few years later, long after we'd gone out of business. He left his widow a substantial fortune. I'm sure he never lied to a customer. On the other hand, I doubt if he ever gave much away, either.

One day, my partner was attending to a little old lady who had walked in. All of a sudden he got up and came over to me.

"Look at this."

He showed me a five-pound note issued by the British Mandatory government in 1947. It looked as though it had come right off the printing press, except that it had been folded four times, to fit inside the old lady's purse.

"She says that after the war, she had saved 40 pounds to buy a sewing machine, and hid the money in a safe place, and then forgot where she'd hidden it. Then yesterday, while she was dusting a bookshelf, the money fell out of the pages of a book. She took one of the bills to the bank across the street, to change it into notes she could use, but they told her it's not legal money any more. They sent her over to us, saying we might give her something for it. What shall I offer her for it?"

Banknotes of the British Mandate are rare, and much sought after by collectors. A crisp, brand-new one like this is very rare indeed.

"Offer her 500 for this one, because it's folded. And tell her that if she brings the others **without folding them, for heaven's sake**, we'll give her 700 for each one. Creasing them reduces their value."

The lady went off happily clutching her 500 lira, saying she'd come back the next day with the others. We never saw her again.

A year or two later, we heard the rest of the story from a customer who knew her. When the old lady got home, and told her son what had happened, he took the banknotes and scoured the length and breadth of the country, till he found a dealer who would give 720 lira for each of them.

If we'd told her the notes were worthless, and offered her twenty lira for the lot, we'd have had them all the next day. The one we did buy from her, we sold for something like 800 lira. The uncreased ones would probably have fetched a thousand apiece --- more, at an auction overseas.

We knew a great deal about coins and banknotes. What we didn't know enough about, was how to conduct a profitable business.

After two years, Anselmo and I were broke, and dissolved our partnership. I was in need of a job. By that time, my Nemesis at the Paper Mill had moved on, and up. The man who had replaced him was an old friend and supporter of mine. I went to see him and said: "I'm broke, and need a job. Will you take me on?"   He said "yes, start tomorrow." He had a high opinion of me, as I had of him, and we got along very well.   I loved him and I wept bitterly when he died. He died suddenly after only a few years.

I worked at that Paper Mill from 1960 to1974, and then from 1976 to 1994 --- a total of 32 years. When I resigned to go into business, I had renounced all my seniority; so my seniority began from zero, at the age of 48. By the time I retired, I had 16 years accumulated, so I haven't much of a pension. My wife Kate supports me now.

7. The death of Zara

All her life Zara used to get tired easily, and she never knew why. She told me that ever since her childhood, she had found that she lost her breath very easily. Training on the farm in England, where working hard was an ideal, getting tired was frowned on. She was sometimes reproached, and even accused of malingering. "Sometimes," she told me, "I didn't even have the strength to ride a bicycle." She never knew why. She lived with this, all through our time in the kibbutz --- until 1968, when she was 36 years old. A few months after the Six-Day War, three of us took a tour of Sinai --- Zara, our son Rafi (then aged 8), and I.

The tour was organized by the Israel Society for the Protection of Nature. We took our own rations, rode in a truck equipped with wooden benches, and slept in tents. The conditions were Spartan, but we had a marvelous time. We visited the oases in Wadi Firan; we reached St. Catherine's Monastery, and Mt. Sinai. When we got to the foot of Mt. Horeb, our guide said "Now, we're going to make the climb to the top." Zara said aside to me: "I can't do this." Rafi said "I want to go to the top," so we sent him off with the guide and the others, and he went to the top --- the same place where Rabbi Goren blew the *shofar* later (he was *Major-General* Rabbi Goren then, Chief Rabbi of the IDF, when he had himself flown to the top of Mt. Sinai and blew his *shofar* there).

Zara said "I can't go another step." There was a Beduin there with a *finjan,* so I bought us a cup of coffee each, and we waited for the others to come back down.   There was a doctor on the trip; he examined Zara, and said to her "what are you doing about that heart murmur?" She replied "I haven't got a heart murmur," and he said "Oh, yes, you have." Nobody had ever told her about that before. Doctors in Israel wear stethoscopes, but they don't always use them. It's a mark of status, like a badge, which identifies a doctor in any Israeli hospital; all of the doctors, and *only* the doctors, wear them. This doctor said "the minute you get home, get them to send you to the heart clinic."

Which we did, of course. That was how we learned that Zara had mitral stenosis. The doctors said it was almost certainly the result of undiagnosed rheumatic fever in childhood.   Rheumatic fever attacks cartilage, and the commonest after-effect of rheumatic fever is a faulty heart valve. Zara had a faulty mitral valve that was leaking very badly; she had a very severe circulatory deficiency. They kept her under surveillance at the heart clinic for several years --- far too long. One day, she went for a routine checkup, and there was a new doctor. He examined her and said "why haven't you had this operated on?" She replied: "no one told me to." He said "you should have had this done ten years ago."

Zara had got to the point, at this time, where the only friends we were visiting were those who lived on the ground floor; she couldn't manage a single flight of stairs. When she went into hospital for the operation, she was asked if she wanted an artificial mitral valve. She replied: "No, thanks, I'd rather keep the bits of plastic out of my body. Just fix up whatever is in there, as well as you can." The surgeon was brilliant; he repaired that valve perfectly, and she came out of that operation a fit, normally functioning woman.

"Now," said Zara, "I want to go on a holiday. I want to travel abroad. I want to do all the things I couldn't do for the last ten years." A few months after the operation, we went on a trip to Spain. In Seville, alongside the Cathedral, there is a tall tower, called the Giralda, built centuries ago by the Moors. It has a spiral ramp, instead of a staircase, leading to the top. Zara said "I'm going to the top of this tower," and we climbed the ramp together.

When we got to the top of the tower, she danced a little dance. It was a very powerful moment. She said "I feel as though I've been born again."   And for the following ten years, for the first time since childhood, Zara was able to lead a fully active life.

~~~~~~~~~~~~~~~~~~~~~

What killed Zara eventually was a glioma --- a primary tumor of the brain. The signs began to appear in mid-1989. It was obvious that she was sick with something.   It didn't occur to anybody, at first, that it was in her brain.   Various doctors thought there was something wrong with her spine, something wrong with her kidneys --- she saw a whole string of specialists.   She was getting progressively worse; her memory started deteriorating.   She would phone me up and say "I seem to be in Hadera, but I'm lost. I can't remember where I've put the car." And I'd have to go to Hadera to find her, and recover the car.

Zara's heart, in the meantime, had completely recovered.   She had lived ten years of perfect health.   As it happened, it was her cardiologist who first had an inkling of what was wrong with her. He sent her for a CT brain scan.   The Hillel Yaffe Hospital in Hadera had, at that time, one of the best brain specialists in the country. He saw the brain scan, and sent urgently for Zara: within 48 hours, she was in surgery. Afterwards, the surgeon said to me "We've taken out as much of the growth as we can. When she comes round, I don't know if she'll be paralyzed, whether she'll be able to speak, or see, or whether she's even going to be conscious."

When Zara finally did regain consciousness, she was able to recover physical motion, she was lucid, she could talk and move; she had no serious motor problems. The surgeon said she had a Grade 3 or 4 glioma --- the worst. "It grows back. We couldn't remove all of it, and within a few months she'll probably be dead." Zara had made me promise to tell her everything the doctors said. When I kept my promise, her comment was; "No doctor's going to tell me how long to live."

In the event, she lived almost three years. She also made me promise not to put her in a hospital, or in any other institution. "I want to die at home," she said. I was able to keep that promise too --- thanks to the help of a large band of wonderful people: friends, doctors, nurses, social workers, who did all they could to make life easier for Zara. Our boys were very good. By that time, both of them lived in Jerusalem: despite their freethinking upbringing, they had become Orthodox Jews, and were married, with small children of their own. There came a time when Zara no longer had the strength to travel to Jerusalem; so every week, each on a different afternoon of the week, one of the boys would come and visit her, bringing one or two of the older grandchildren (aged from about five to nine) with him. The journey, by buses and cabs, took about three-and-a-half hours each way, and the visit would last a couple of hours. The grandchildren remember those visits vividly, to this day. They came in all weathers, and were a great comfort to Zara.

Zara and I were married for 42 years. I consider myself a very lucky man to have shared those years with her.

~~~~~~~~~~~~~~~~~~~~~~

Excerpts from an occasional diary kept by Zara during her illness:

In Edinburgh, in summer, it is still light at 10 o'clock at night – light enough to play tennis. We would be playing in the garden in the evening, and then: "it's time for Zara to go to bed." I'd watch, and hear the boys enjoying themselves --- my day was over, while everybody else could continue having fun. I had to get to bed and go to sleep.

265

Now, fifty years later, I have a similar feeling. I'm dying --- my life is almost over, and everyone that I know is going to continue living. Again I'm cheated. How did this happen to me?

****

In 1948 the State of Israel came into being. This large family of mine decided to ignore the event. For me, it was a perfect opportunity to escape.

My husband, my sons and I have lived in Israel since 1953. My only disappointment is that no other member of the family has decided to settle in Israel. Now --- how I long to be surrounded by my brothers, their wives, and children. How I long for their visits. Life is always the wrong way round.

****

About a year and a half ago, very weird things began to happen to me. I kept on falling down, I lost my sense of balance, my ears hurt me, I couldn't hear properly. I couldn't see out of one eye. My memory was really weird --- I'd ask the same question ten times in a quarter of an hour. Each time, I'd get an answer, but I'd immediately forget it. Once I fell down a flight of steps. After that, we reckoned that all my problems came from the damage the fall had done to my spine. We now had an X-ray, to show the damage.

During all this time, I had the most terrible headaches. I lost my coordination. I couldn't dial the telephone, tie my shoelaces or fix my brassiere. ---- There was one day when I visited three doctors, looking for the root of my problems.

Eventually, I was sent to have a C.T. scan. This showed I had a brain tumour. This isn't exactly good news, but it was an explanation that I could understand. The six months before had been inexplicable suffering.

****

DOCTORS AND DOCTORS.

I have a malignant brain tumour. For a year I have been tested, operated on, radiated, and dosed with chemicals. Immediately after the operation, a doctor told my husband that I had twelve months to live, and during that time I would feel progressively worse - a very depressing prognosis. After making this statement, the doctor went away, leaving a shocked family to cope with this prospect as best they might.

I tried to work out my future. It was then I decided

to try and find a more sympathetic medical adviser. After some time, and by great good fortune, I found one. He listened to my sad tale and said: "I can't promise you a cure --but I can improve the quality of your life. If you are willing to fight this, I will fight along beside you. Let us start as soon as possible."

One doctor began our first (and only) interview by examining my file -- a business that took about three-quarters of an hour. Then he glanced at me and asked me how I was. During the interview he asked me: "Who is the Prime Minister of Israel?" Seeing my surprise at this question (I am a middle-aged woman, not a child) he explained that he wanted to know what kind of person he had to deal with. I was sorry not to have answered "Genghis Khan"' or "Moses."

My first interview with another doctor was quite different. He didn't look at my file; he looked at me. He watched how I moved, walked, hung up my coat --- then asked me about the history of my illness. How did I feel? What were the first symptoms? How had my condition progressed? He was interested in my reactions to this dreadful illness. Only after this did he spend a few minutes looking at my file.

To one doctor, I was not a person, but an illness recorded in the file. He treated me because I carried the illness around with me. To the other doctor, I was first of all a human being, who needed help because I had this malignant tumour.

The operation, radiation and chemotherapy combined to rid me of all the hair on my head. When I mention how this distresses me, one doctor replies: "Wait until the end of treatment, then we'll see." It doesn't seem to strike him that if I wait till the end of treatment, I could be dead before my hair starts to grow. Another doctor listens to my complaint, and suggests a course of vitamins, to begin immediately. He says: "It may not help much, but it's worth trying."

One doctor gives an offhand reply --- the other listens, then gives a properly thought-out answer. When I complain of burns around my ear from the radiation, one doctor says: "Yes, well - maybe you should see a skin doctor." The other says: "Try this ointment. It's very good for burns." He makes his work much easier by listening to what his patient says ---- and, of course, I also believe that he is taking better care of me.

This same doctor doesn't wait for me to ask questions. He explains the reasons for the treatment I am getting. It makes me feel we are working together to make me better. I feel I can trust him. I cannot feel this way when I am simply the passive recipient of whatever treatment the doctor decides to give me.

****

The operation was set for December 3rd [*1990.— Ed.*] —my birthday. All the tests had been completed and I had been anesthetized; all was ready ---then, crowds of people seemed to fill the operating theatre, together with TV cameras. What was this? Then I was told that there had been an attack [*by terrorists.---Ed.*] on a civilian bus, and the injured had been brought to "my" hospital for emergency treatment. No operation for me that day.

The next day, Dec 4th, I was anesthetized again --- the first time in the hospital's history that a patient was gassed twice for the same operation. Again, a series of tests ---what kind of tumour was it? The headaches had gone; I felt much better, even though it had been impossible to remove all the growth without removing half my brain.

We were informed that I had about a year to live --- during which time I'd feel progressively worse.

This seemed so sad --- we decided to look for less conventional treatment.

I continued with the usual, conventional treatment --- radiation, chemotherapy --- while starting a course of homeopathic, non-toxic medicine at a clinic in Holland. This I am still continuing in my home town in Israel.

My two sons are studying at religious colleges in Jerusalem --- they have been praying for me since my illness was discovered.

****

I try everything that can help me ---- are they all helping me, or is one form of treatment responsible for the fact that I'm still alive, looking and feeling quite well?

As the wise women say --- it helps that my husband loves me, and does everything in his power to help me.   He makes sure I don't miss a pill or a treatment. If I had two hearts I could love him more.

When I first became ill, before we knew exactly what was wrong, my sons and their wives looked after me when my husband's work absented him from Israel. They saved a life (my sons are fine young men, who know how to love --- and their wives are wonderful).

When I came home from Holland [....and needed injections and electric treatment three times a week (brain tumour patients can't drive, and I live in an outlying neighbourhood of a small country town --- Hadera) friends arranged a duty-rota, to take me to and from the clinic; I never had to bother about it ---- they arranged it all. Friends have made sure I'm not isolated --- they visit. It can't be too cheerful for them......They come for supper, bringing supper with them ---- and enough food for the rest of the week. We've never eaten so well in all our lives. I've put on weight. Best of all --- while I was still in hospital, my brothers, their wives and children --- all adults now --- have visited and helped me. It's great good luck to be a member of a large family.

It's not always cheerful to be in my company --- I'm inclined to spend too much time talking about treatments, doctors, the management --- or lack of it --- in our major hospitals. Some people can't stand being in the presence of approaching death. Others can't say the words --- cancer, tumour, growth. I'm disappointed with such lack of courage --- it's inclined to isolate me.

There are many subjects and occupations that no longer interest me. Shopping used to be a pleasant way of spending a morning when at home, or a day when I was abroad --- now, I shop for the food we need for the week. I used to love TV --- almost every evening, I'd sit hypnotized by the programmes. Now, I've no patience for it --- almost every TV show bores me. I've gone back to reading, day and night.

....

"By saving one soul ---- you save the world."

****

As a result of radiation therapy my hair fell out. This made me particularly miserable when I looked in the mirror. The wig-maker in Hadera has made me three wigs --- all different. He looks after them for me, shampooing, setting, spraying with rosemary. It makes me feel good, dealing with such a caring, sympathetic person. My first wig was paid for 1/3 by the National Insurance, 1/3 by the Anti-Cancer League, and 1/3 by me. Now, Eli the wig maker....... [*Here the manuscript ends. ---Ed.*]

■■■

8. Elvira and the *Conversos*

My maternal grandfather, Henry Edward Hurst, was born in England in 1852, and at a very early age was taken with his family to Valparaiso, Chile, where he spent most of his life. From his father, Henry Hunt Hurst (an English engineer and industrialist), he inherited a business in Valparaiso. It had to do with the import and export of iron and possibly other materials too, and had a *barraca,* or warehouse, downtown, somewhere near the port area.

At some time during the 1880's Henry Edward Hurst married a Chilean lady. This was an unusual thing for an expatriate English gentleman to do at that time. There was a considerable Anglo-Chilean community in and around Valparaiso. Most of the country's trade with Europe was handled by British companies, with names like Duncan, Fox & Co., Williamson, Balfour, & Co., Gibbs & Co., etc., and carried on British ships, belonging to companies such as the Pacific Steam Navigation Company, which operated a fleet of cargo and passenger vessels. And the people who ran these companies' operations in Chile were Britons. British people living in Chile formed a close, exclusive community; their children (boys, at any rate) were sent to school in England. I know that Henry Edward Hurst attended either Cambridge or Oxford University. Even after having been settled in Chile for two, or even three generations, Anglo-Chileans were very much segregated from the Chilean population.

Some of my school friends at St. Peter's during the 1940's, who had never seen England --- and whose parents might very well never have seen it either--- would refer to England as "Home." Even though Chile was a sovereign state, the attitude of most members of the Anglo-Chilean community toward Chileans, was much like the attitude of Britons throughout the British Empire toward the subject peoples they ruled. There was an automatic assumption of superiority (a superiority conferred, of course, by God Almighty, *"beneath whose awful hand we hold / dominion over palm and pine"*). Chileans weren't much better --- if at all --- than the brown, black, and yellow nations of the Empire. To associate with them was necessarily to condescend; actually to marry one, would be to demean oneself. It happened only rarely. My sister-in-law Ruby's grandfather, Bertram Brice, married a Chilean lady..... but he was a wealthy and powerful man, who did as he pleased, and cared not a bit for what others said, or thought. So when Henry Edward Hurst married a Chilean in the 1880's, he wasn't doing "the done thing." Very much not.

This may be one of the reasons that we know so very little about her. Families tend to keep quiet about the oddities in their midst – especially about those which are even mildly disreputable. We know that after the Hurst home in Valparaiso was destroyed by the great earthquake of 1906, Henry Edward sent his wife --- whom he called "Elvira" --- and several of their children (including my mother)to England for a while; and we know, from surviving correspondence, that the English Hursts gave Elvira a hard time.

But until fairly recently, we knew practically nothing more. My cousin Edmund and his mother lived with Henry Edward and Elvira for a while, shortly after World War 1. Edmund was a small boy at the time. He told me that all he remembered of Elvira was that she had a fierce temper, and that when she was angry about anything, it was a good idea to stay out of her way. Edmund died some years ago.

A renewed family interest in Elvira and her origins was stimulated some years ago, by certain events involving my family, here in Israel. This is the story: My wife Zara was Jewish, and our children were therefore also Jewish (since Jewish identity is transmitted, in Jewish law, only by matrilinear descent). I, on the other hand, was not. This was of no importance while Zara was alive. We lived as a secular Jewish family. Zara and I were both freethinkers. Whether or not I was technically a Jew, made no difference to us, nor to our friends and acquaintances.

When both our sons underwent a religious rebirth in the 1980's, and became strictly Orthodox Jews, nothing changed in the relations between us. The Fifth Commandment, "honour thy father and thy mother," overrides all others, except for the four which precede it. Our sons continued to show Zara and me the same filial love and respect as always, despite the fact that Jewish religious law strictly forbids a Jew to marry a non-Jew, under penalty of exclusion from the community. We remained a close knit family. The fact of my technically not being Jewish was not concealed from our grandchildren.

I remember once I was walking in Ben Yehuda Street with two of my grandchildren, each one with *payot* (long sidelocks). Suddenly a man came rushing out of a house, saw me and begged me to make up a minyan. Being honest, I whispered that I was not Jewish. The man looked at me astonished, walking with two Haredi children, and made a sign showing that he thought I was mad and disappeared.

Here are a couple of small incidents from that time –they may throw a little light on the social climate in which these children were growing up: It was early December. Joshua, aged 8 or 9, was visiting Zara and me with his parents, and saw me writing Christmas cards to some relatives and friends.

"What are you doing, Saba?" (*Saba* means "Grandpa")

"I am sending greeting cards to some of my Christian cousins; it will soon be Christmas, an important holiday for them – like New Year for us."

"You have Christian cousins, Saba?"

"Yes, of course. And so do you --- my cousins are your cousins, too, remember."

He thought about this, it had evidently never occurred to him before.

"Christians believe in Jesus, don't they, Saba?"

"That's right."

"Do you believe in Jesus?"

"No. I did once, when I was a little boy; but I stopped believing long, long ago."   He went away pondering these new ideas very thoughtfully indeed.

One day I was on a visit to my son Raphael and his family in Jerusalem.   Little Shachar, aged about eight, came close to me.

"Saba, will you do something if I ask you?"

"Of course, my dear, if I can. What is it?"

"When you talk to Moshe's friends, please don't tell them you're not Jewish."   [Moshe is Shachar's brother, then aged about six]

"Of course I won't, since you've asked me not to. Why do you ask?"

"Because if they know you're not Jewish, they might not want to play with him any more."   A non-Jew in the family is not a social asset in those very strict Orthodox circles (a *bona fide* convert to Judaism, on the other hand, is treated with special respect, since he is a volunteer, whereas born Jews are, so to speak, conscripts).   Nowadays my grandchildren are growing up and getting married. I do not discuss my antecedents with their spouses, or their spouses' families--- If they choose to do so, that is their concern.

After Zara's death in August, 1993, everything changed......When Zara and I were married, she was 18 years old, I was 21. We were married for 42 years. After her death, I found widowhood a very unsatisfactory state to be in, and soon began looking for a way out of it. My attention focused on Kate. We had been friends for over thirty years: she and her husband were frequent visitors to our house. During Zara's illness, they were divorced. Zara said to each of them: "If you're not going to visit me together any more, I'd like both of you to continue visiting me separately." And so it was: both of them continued to visit regularly, for the rest of Zara's life – what little was left of it.

Kate was no more content with being single than was I. A few months after Zara's death, we began to explore the possibility of sharing our lives. We visited my children in Jerusalem together a couple of times. Then the lightning-bolt fell......One of my sons asked me not to bring Kate to visit his home. I was thunderstruck. - *Why?*
"Kate is Jewish – you are not. It is forbidden for her to marry, or to cohabit with, a non-Jew. And if she does so, even with you, we cannot accept her in our home." From my second son, I heard the same. I had done nothing wrong: the commandments of the Torah apply only to a Jew.

They applied to Kate. I was forbidden to her, and if she chose me as a mate, she could not come into their home.

"Why are you only now telling me this? How come you didn't do this to your mother?"

"Because she was our mother, different rules apply. Kate is not our mother: we cannot accept her." This was appalling.

Kate and I discussed the situation at length. I was furious. "If I can't bring you with me when I visit, I shan't visit them at all." Not so fast, said Kate. "Are you seriously going to cut yourself off from your grandchildren? What have they done to you, that you should deprive them of a grandfather? What if, one day, they need you? Of course you must continue to visit them. And if you must go alone --- so be it. Go alone."

That was eventually what I did. And each time I went, it was like being divorced. Time did nothing to lessen the pain and distress which we both felt. My children, I know, were distressed too. They are loving children, and had no desire to hurt either of us. When the Jews returned to Israel from their Babylonian exile, 2500 years ago, many of them had non-Jewish wives. Ezra and Nehemiah offered them a choice: put away your non-Jewish wives, and join us in rebuilding the Temple --- or keep your wives, in which case you will be excluded from the Jewish community, and have no share in the Temple.

It felt as though nothing much had changed.

Kate refused to take the situation lying down. "What makes you so certain you're not Jewish?" she asked me. "What about that story you told me?" The story to which she alluded was as follows: When I was a boy, my mother once told me: "You can drink milk before you eat meat – but don't ever drink milk after you've eaten meat."

"Why not?"

"Because it's bad for you. It'll make you ill."

"Who told you that?"

"My mother."

I always remembered this, because it seemed such an odd thing to say. I had no notion at the time – nor for many years thereafter – that my mother was quoting Jewish dietary law. Neither did my mother, who all her life was a believing Christian, though not much of a churchgoer. One day when I told this story to my daughter-in-law Nita, she laughed and said: "Somewhere deep down, you are a Jew, *Saba* --- I'm sure of it!"

Kate wouldn't let this go. She began to make inquiries, and drew me after her--- into a chapter of history, many centuries long and not yet ended, which grew ever more fascinating, the deeper we went into it. Jews have lived in Spain for a very long time – but it was under the Moslem rulers of Spain that Jews fared best. Moslems are required by Islamic law to tolerate Jews and Christians, and to allow them to live peaceably in their midst (albeit as second-class citizens – *dhimmi* -- subject to a variety of restrictions, taxes, and humiliations). In those parts of the Iberian peninsula under Moslem rule, from the 7th century C.E. onwards, Jews found themselves a lot better off than under any mediaeval Christian government.

Jews eventually came to form an important sector of the Spanish population, numerically, culturally and economically. However, the Christians, unwavering in their determination to reconquer the peninsula, fought back century after century, gradually driving the Moslems back; and in those lands which returned to Christian rule, Jews found themselves in a very uncomfortable situation indeed. The pressure on Jews to convert to Christianity was relentless: forced baptisms were common, often performed publicly and *en masse.* Many Jews were killed for their obstinate refusal to renounce their religion. Those who accepted Christianity found that their troubles were not over --- on the contrary, they'd just begun. "New Christians," or *Conversos* as converted Jews were called, were watched very closely: the slightest hint of Judaic practice could lead to a charge of heresy, which was severely punishable --- often, by torture and death.

The Christian reconquest of Spain was completed in 1492, with the fall of Granada. In the same year, Columbus discovered America, and Their Catholic Majesties Ferdinand and Isabella issued the Edict of Expulsion. All Jews remaining in the kingdom must either leave the kingdom by a certain date, or accept baptism – or be put to death. Many Jews went to Portugal (from whence they were expelled a few years later). Many went to other Mediterranean countries, including the Turkish domains. There is no agreement among historians as to the numbers involved: numbers in the hundreds of thousands are mentioned. Many remained in Spain, and accepted baptism. These last immediately came under the scrutiny of the Spanish Inquisition, set up under Royal authority around 1480.

The Inquisition's function was to discover heretics, and try to bring them back to the True Faith. Despite the Inquisition's zeal, which provided regular public spectacles (called *auto-da-fe* or "Acts of Faith") at which New Christians found guilty of Judaizing were burned alive, many converted Jews continued to practice the religion of their fathers in secret, while maintaining an outer semblance of Christianity.

Columbus' discovery of America provided these last with a splendid opportunity. The Spanish government was interested in colonizing its new "Empire of the Indies," and gave encouragement, and sometimes help, to those prepared to settle there, without always enquiring too closely into their credentials. And the Inquisition was far too busy with its work in Spain, to pay much attention to what was going on in the distant peripheral colonies. It did not even begin operations in Latin America till almost the end of the 16th century, and didn't get really warmed up for another hundred years after that.

There is little doubt that many of the Spanish families who settled in South America were New Christians, seeking to escape the attentions of the Inquisition. Obviously they could not organize any

Jewish religious activity, for fear of disclosure; and they tended to intermarry with other *converso* families rather than with Old Christians, who often regarded them with suspicion, and even with hostility. In the course of time, their knowledge and understanding of Judaism declined, and only vestiges of Jewish practice remained. These vestiges can be observed to this day, all over Latin America. There are (Christian) families where the mother lights two candles on Friday night, because *her* mother taught her to do so. Families which eat their dessert (which may contain cream) before eating their main meal, which might include meat. Families where a mother advises her daughter never to drink milk after eating meat, because it may do her harm.

The more we looked into the matter, the more significant this odd remark of my mother's appeared to become. There were plenty of sources of information; in recent years, interest in the history of these converted Jews has greatly increased, among both Jews and non-Jews. Racial attitudes have begun to change in the Western world; having Jewish (or Amerindian, or Asian, or African) ancestors in your family tree is no longer necessarily something you try desperately to keep secret. A Spanish Prime Minister recently boasted of his Jewish ancestors. People all over the Christian world are rediscovering their Jewish roots. Entire communities have been discovered, in Portugal,, such as Belmonte, of "Crypto-Jews" --- people who, outwardly practicing Christianity, attending church and having their children baptized, have for hundreds of years secretly maintained many features of Jewish ritual practice and worship.

Our friend Ignacio Steinhardt, a world-known expert on, and student of, the Portuguese crypto-Jews, helped Kate and me a great deal, providing information concerning a subject about which we initially knew nothing, and referring us to additional sources. Other friends directed us to *Casa Shalom*, a non-profit organization in Israel, headed by Mrs. Gloria Mound, which is helping many Jews rediscover a forgotten heritage.
"Let us see what we can find out" said Kate.

We began with names. Names are important. Semitic peoples, unlike Europeans, didn't go in much for surnames. A Jew in medieval Spain would simply call himself Isaac ben Abraham, say, or Moses ben Maimon. But on becoming a Christian, he would be required to take a surname. Lopez. Contreras. Diaz. For some reason, Jews seemed to prefer certain surnames over others: perhaps as markers, to help other *conversos* identify them. The fact is, that there are lists of surnames – a hundred or so – which occur over and over again among known *converso* families.

Contreras – my grandmother's paternal surname -- is one of them. Díaz is another. Rosario ("Charo") Díaz was the name of my mother's unmarried Chilean cousin, who used to come and visit us in Villa Alemana from time to time. My mother didn't particularly like her: once in conversation, I referred to her as "Aunt Charo."
"Don't call her that!" said my mother, visibly annoyed. "She's *not* your aunt.
She's only my cousin." I think Charo received a small pension from the Chilean Navy, on account of someone in her family who'd served in it. I don't know anything else about her; and there's nobody left to ask.

All we had so far was two surnames. "Let's see if we can find more," said Kate. She travelled to Chile on other business; and while there, she did what she could to see if any official records were available, and if so, what they had to say. Official bodies --- the authorities at Valparaiso's Cemetery No, 1, where Henry Edward and his wife are buried; the *Registro Civil*; the Municipality of Valparaíso --- were all willing to help, as far as they could. This is what Kate was finally able to uncover:

Elvira's name was not "Elvira." This was, presumably, a pet name used by her husband, and possibly by others in her family. On her death certificate, dated October 28, 1926, the given names are recorded as "Isabel Salmira." Since she died two years after Henry Edward, it could not have been he who gave these details to the registrar (there is no birth certificate -- in 1860, when she was born, there was as yet no *Registro Civil* in Chile). There is no evident Jewish connection. Daughters of *converso* families were often, though not invariably, given two names.

The names of "Elvira"'s parents were recorded on her death certificate. They are José María Contreras and Tomasa Mendoza. Here we are on firmer ground. Of all the surnames preferred by Jews converted to Christianity, "Mendoza" is one of those most frequently met. It is also fairly common among Jews who left Spain at the Expulsion, and settled in other countries.

Kate tried to find further information about Tomasa Mendoza, and succeeded in coming up with a copy of her death certificate: she died, a widow, in 1893, about seven years after the opening of the *Registro Civil*. The death certificate gives her name as *"Tomasa Mendoza viuda* (widow) *de Contreras,"* and her age at time of death as seventy years (i.e. she was born around 1823). Under "Names of Parents" the handwritten entry is: *no se informa* or possibly *no se expresa* --- "no information given." The Registrar told Kate that early in the 19th century, many marrying couples preferred not to identify their parents by name. The Inquisition had shut down only a few years earlier; and if they were from families that might possibly be suspect, the less anyone knew about their antecedents, the better. It is possible that at the time of Tomasa's death, no one living --- not even her children --- knew the names of her parents.

The only place left, at which to make inquiries about births and deaths, was the *Obispado* (Bishopric) of Valparaíso. They were very friendly --- but there was nothing more useful they could tell us. This appeared to be about as far as we could go.

"It looks quite clear to me" said Chaim. "With all those surnames in the family --- and with that little story about the milk --- it's clear to me that your grandmother must have been descended from a Jewish family. A strict *Beth Din* (Jewish religious court) might consider it doubtful, and ask you to undergo a token conversion (*giyur besafek)* for form's sake; but there's no doubt in my mind. You're a Jew." Raphael was of the same view. So -- in their opinion, my grandmother was Jewish. It followed from this that my mother Jane was Jewish, too, and so were all her siblings --- my Auntie Berta (also Berta's children, George and Albert) and my Uncles Harry and Charlie --- and all my mother's children: my brothers Larry and Ron, and myself.

Well, as far as I am concerned, nothing could be better. It means that Kate's marriage to me is a proper and lawful one, in Jewish law (and also that Zara's was likewise, long ago, though we didn't know it at the time) --- and that there are no longer any barriers to our living in a normal, happy family relationship not only with each other, which we've always done, but with all of each other's children as well. It has removed a terrible, painful strain from all our lives; and it shows what a determined, intelligent woman is capable of, when she finds her happiness at stake, and makes up her mind that action is called for.

"Eshet hayil mi yimtza?" says the Book of Proverbs. "Who will find a good woman? For her value is above rubies." My own feelings entirely.

Author's note

I met Elliott Hurst in 1963 on our first visit to Israel. We had been given the Hurst's address in Hadera to look up by my cousin Sheila, who had been a member of their original *garin*. She and her husband Leslie had been forced to return to England when their son became very ill.   She kindly wrote a letter to the Hursts for us, but we had no idea whether or not they would welcome us as guests. I had organized a group of 8 people to travel to Israel in a mini-bus (I have described this trip in my story "*The Grand Tour*" in my collection "*Trove*"). After landing in Haifa we had gone our separate ways for a while.

My wife and I arrived in Hadera by bus in the early evening and wandered around (without smart phones, or even a map) searching for their address, an apartment on Hagiborim Street.   As dusk approached we saw a group of people standing around by a door that was lit as they were apparently leaving. I approached them and in my terrible Hebrew asked if they could direct us. In response I got a reply in heavily accented Scottish English, "Ah, you'll be looking for the Hursts." "Do you know them?" I asked with incredulity. "Aye,

Zara Hurst works for me, Hadera is only a wee town." After we had introduced ourselves, he ushered us in as their guests left and invited us to join them for a cup of tea.

He introduced himself as John McDonald and told us his story, he had been one of the two British soldiers who had defected to the *Haganah* during the War of Independence in 1948 and had brought their tanks over with them. This was a great prize for the Jewish fighting force which had no heavy weapons. He had met a beautiful Jewish girl (love is often the motivation) and once he had deserted they married and he had to stay in Israel. Only a few years earlier he had visited the UK and been given permission to do so without fear of arrest. We spoke to his wife and daughter, a Scottish-Israeli. Meanwhile he went off and phoned the Hursts, and eventually Elliott came over and collected us.

They were perfect hosts and we greatly enjoyed our brief stay with them. I was particularly struck by Elliott, he made a strong impression on me. He described how he had come from Chile to England, joined a *Habonim garin* and had married Zara, and they had lived on a *kibbutz*. He was Israeli but he was not Jewish, and had no intention of converting since he was an atheist. He explained his socialist beliefs to me, but admitted how these had not stood up to practice in the *kibbutz*. He was very well read and knowledgeable and I found him to be extremely intelligent, in fact one of the most intelligent people I had ever met. We sat up talking well into the night.

Later, in the 1960s and again in the 1970s when we lived in Israel, first when I was a student and then on sabbatical, we re-established contact with the Hursts and visited them in their new house and they in turn visited us for lunch in Rehovot. However, his son, while playing in our large unkempt front yard, unfortunately disturbed a nest of wasps and was badly stung. So the visit was cut short and they rushed him off to the clinic. We had no further contact for ca. 43 years.

Then I was at a party at a friend's house in Los Angeles in about 1990. I was speaking to my friend's *machatunim* (son's in-law) who had just returned from a trip to Israel and he was a serious coin collector, and he mentioned that he had bought some Roman coins from an Elliott Hurst in Haifa, perhaps I knew him. I asked, "is it the same Elliott Hurst who used to live in Hadera?" and he replied "I don't know, how many Elliott Hursts can there be in Israel." I was so amazed, I wanted to get in touch with him, but there was no Elliott Hurst listed in the Haifa telephone book and I never followed up.

Then one night about a year ago I was unable to sleep and I finally googled "Elliott Hurst and Roman coins" and I got a hit. It was a coin dealer in Wales and he gave me Elliott's direct e-mail address. So I wrote to Elliott out of the blue, and received a reply the next day. We met soon after and then he kindly sent me some of his memoirs, but they were all in disjointed sections. I proposed to edit them and make a coherent story out of it, and at Elliott's 85th birthday party he agreed that I should do that. That was the genesis of this work.

Madrich's Note

I met Elliott in 1949 when a fellow student at Liverpool University, brought him to Beit Habonim where I was the *Madrich* (leader) of the Liverpool members. Habonim was a Jewish Scouting movement which was founded in 1929, but had become a Zionist Youth movement whose chaverim (members) had strong leanings to eventually emigrate to Israel and live in *kibbutzim*. In no time this non-Jewish young man from Chile joined the movement and became fascinated with the idea of becoming a *kibbutznik*. Strangely enough, he later came to live in Israel whilst his girlfriend remained in England, where she died at the ripe old age of 80.

In 1950 Elliott approached me together with a fellow student named Mike whose home was in Southport and who was also a member of *Habonim*. At that time *Beit Habonim* was a large former home. Elliott and Mike asked if they could come and live there, using one of the empty rooms. By that time I was married and my wife agreed that they could come and live there and she would worry about their meals and laundry.

Although Mike was a very serious student, we hardly noticed when Elliott would attend lectures at the university. He was an unusually clever lad who apparently managed to get by, by reading only. Finally he had to take his last examination for which he prepared by reading in his bath no less than eight hours. The next morning we had to schlep him out of bed and send him on his way on the back of a chaver's motorcycle, otherwise he would have missed his finals. He passed quite easily. In the summer the Secretariat of *Habonim* sent him on a six week course to learn Hebrew. So we had a situation where a non-Jewish boy from Chile knew Hebrew better than the majority of *chaverim* in the movement.

In the course of time he went on *Hachshara* - a preparatory course where *chaverim* learnt to live together in a kibbutz framework. He went on *aliya* (going to live in Israel) to Kibbutz Amiad where he met and married Zara who was from Edinburgh and became the one and only non-Jewish man who became a Secretary of a kibbutz.

Elliott and Zara had two sons with whom they lived in Hadera when they left the kibbutz. After leaving the kibbutz Elliott worked for more than thirty years for the Hadera Paper Mills as its biochemist, with a remarkably low salary. Nevertheless, his expertise in paper making is such that he is asked, until this very day at the ripe old age of 85, to lecture on paper making.

Glossary:

Aliyah: Settling in Israel (in Hebrew literally "going up")

Chaverim: A group of friends

Converso: A Jew forcibly converted to Christianity in Iberia, also called a New Christian or *Marrano or* Crypto-Jew, who practised elements of Judaism secretly

Garin: A group of people preparing for aliyah together (literally "seed" in Hebrew)

Habonim: A socialist Jewish youth movement (literally "the builders")

Hachsharah: Preparation/training to make *aliyah* to a *kibbutz*

Haganah: The Defense Force of the Jewish Labor movement in Palestine, the precursor of the Israeli Army.

Haredi: An ultra-Orthodox Jew, distinguished by wearing black dress and having facial side curls (*payot*)

Hebrew: Ancient language of the Jewish people, in which the Bible is written. Resurrected as a spoken language by Eliezer Ben Yehuda (1858-1922)

IDF: The Israel Defense Force. Israeli Army

Inquisition: An institution of the Catholic Church established in 1478 to root out heretics

within Catholicism, especially among
New Christians (Jews)

Kibbutz: Socialist cooperative farm in Israel

Palmach: The shock troops of the Jewish
settlement in Palestine

Technion: University of science and technology in
Haifa

Zionism: The national liberation movement of the
Jewish people, pioneered by Theodor
Herzl (1860-1904)